BEYOND MEASURE

BEYOND

5.77

2.40

14.68

RACHEL Z. ARNDT

.30

MEASURE

10.37

ESSAYS

SARABANDE BOOKS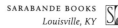
Louisville, KY

Library of Congress Cataloging-in-Publication Data
Names: Arndt, Rachel Z., author.
Title: Beyond measure : essays / by Rachel Z. Arndt.
Description: First edition. | Louisville, KY : Sarabande Books, 2018
Identifiers: LCCN 2017032569 | ISBN 9781946448132 (softcover)
Classification: LCC PS3601.R5787 A6 2018 | DDC 814/.6—dc23
LC record available at https://lccn.loc.gov/2017032569

Cover design by Kristen Radtke.
Interior by Alban Fischer.
Manufactured in Canada.
This book is printed on acid-free paper.
Sarabande Books is a nonprofit literary organization.

  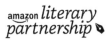

This project is supported in part by an award from the National Endowment for the Arts.
The Kentucky Arts Council, the state arts agency, supports Sarabande Books with state
tax dollars and federal funding from the National Endowment for the Arts.

She woke up sounding the walls of her memory
for particulars

—C. D. WRIGHT

CONTENTS

BEYOND MEASURE

SLEEP

waited in my pajamas—boxers and a T-shirt baggy enough to have wires threaded down the neck and out the bottom. There, they'd connect to a box of terminals, each tiny opening marked with a letter and number, the whole thing very advanced yet also reminiscent of a switchboard or old stereo receiver. I waited for the technician next door in the Electrode Room; I waited on my bed, listening to the muffled conversation between him and my neighbor. I have to hurry, the man explained; my next patient is someone who might have narcolepsy, and she needs to go to sleep soon. I sat on top of the covers reading because under the covers made the pose too familiar, too much like waiting for a man in my own bed.

I had my first sleep study when I was in college: narcolepsy. A couple of years later, in a new city, another: narcolepsy. (Maybe if I say the word enough here it'll become easier to say out there, where most people don't know how to react except with Really? and Are you sure? and I have insomnia too.) Now, living in yet another city, my new doctor wanted confirmation that I had narcolepsy, not some other problem. I could have the test—a night and day spent in a sleep lab—"whenever's convenient," which was never, but which also happened to be during summer break from grad school, when

I could afford to step out of the world for twenty-four hours and into the benevolent but sadistic schedule of a sleep study. In the meantime, my doctor said, I probably shouldn't drive.

When making the appointment, the receptionist on the phone asked what time I usually go to bed, which would determine when I needed to show up. We try to make things as normal as possible for you, she said, and I didn't point out—didn't need to point out—that if it were even remotely similar to normal, I wouldn't be planning on the phone what time I'd be going to sleep.

I told the woman I usually turn in around ten thirty; arriving at the sleep lab by nine would give me plenty of time, she said.

The cautioned-against drive to the Sleep Disorders Center was ten minutes from my house. It took me three minutes to park, six minutes to walk to the building.

I'm here for a sleep study, I told the intercom.

Who are you? the intercom asked.

I was buzzed in. The room, with its familiar wall-mounted camera, greeted me, and the sleep technician quizzed me using the Epworth Sleepiness Scale. He called me Ma'am. He pulled his jeans at the knees as he sat and asked me how likely (3 = very likely, 0 = very unlikely) I was to fall asleep in certain situations, including, among others, "sitting and reading" (3), "sitting inactive in a public place" (1.5), "lying down to rest in the afternoon when circumstances permit" (3).

Night was seeping in. The sandy day gathered itself in traces, windswept. In the sleep study the real night would arrive, then certain sleep. First, in the ebbing and flowing twilight that holds night from day, there was preparation. The technician asked if

I could wait for him to set up someone else's sensor electrodes before mine.

Alone and unable to focus on my book, I eavesdropped. The technician pontificated about women: Men, he said, either fall asleep or they don't. There's no trying to fall asleep for a man, he said. If a man can't fall asleep within ten minutes of lying down, he'll get out of bed and leave the bedroom to be productive elsewhere.

Women, on the other hand, lie in bed worrying, he continued. They worry about what they'll wear the next day and what they'll pack for their kids' lunches.

I worried. And while I worried and waited for the technician to glue on my electrodes, I peered from the bed toward where a painting should be if this were a temporary bedroom (i.e., a hotel room). In place of art, a camera. It was no less beautiful than a hotel-room painting, but neither was it more beautiful. In the footage I'd spend 29 percent of the night on my back and 71 percent on my side, all of it in the green of nausea, all of it bulging in surveillance wide-angle.

I appreciated the window in the room, which added some verisimilitude to the experience. Maybe it would be better to rule out possible diagnoses, to confirm that all we could know about my sleepiness was that it was unknowable. Outside, past the concrete courtyard the window framed, there was a world going on. I texted two friends about going to dinner the next night, after the test—my grand return. I'd wear my new black dress. And, for those few hours, I'd ignore the new trouble rising: that a grand return to routine after not quite leaving the routine isn't grand, and it isn't really a return.

But this was too much, this thinking about people that led to thinking about what those people might be doing without me and if I was missing something by being here, the center of attention. If I didn't stop, I wouldn't be in tip-top shape for sleeping and would fuck up the whole test. So I turned off my phone, tugged at the blinds' two pull-strings individually until the slats fell parallel to the floor, and took in the scenery of the room: The vinyl chairs, the sagging bed, the noisy pillows—those were also problems. They did not fit into the notion of normalcy. This inside world was proving just as troubling as the outside, and I wondered, before the study even began, how well I'd do at performing something habitual in a new but familiar setting, one uncannily like the other sleep labs in shape and intent but, not yet at least, in results. Can one make a diagnosis based on data gathered from a performance? Summoned by the technician, I got up and followed him into the Electrode Room.

The Electrode Room was cold, and the technician wore latex gloves. Outside stood a sign: "Quiet. Sleep test in progress." Inside, I got my costume: wires likes marionette strings from the chest and legs, china marker scratched at precise points on my head, a bright red X on each temple. A tube hung from my ears and looped under my nose. By way of small talk, the technician mentioned that he'd just been in Chicago for his aunt's funeral and, boy, there are just too many traffic lights there. A compressor chugged air against my scalp, solidifying the glue in bursts, the soundscape like a conversation between people who've just met.

In bed and ready for the night, I felt my body against layers of blankets and wires—so much opportunity to become tangled. During my last two sleep studies, electrodes often detached during the night. They must be glued well enough to stay put but not so well as to make them permanent.

I waited beneath the minimal buzzing in the room, now ready for sleep.

Can you hear me? came the sleep technician's voice from somewhere near the camera, beginning the pre-study sensor calibration.

I could hear him, though he couldn't hear me until he entered and fiddled with something in the Electrode Room.

Can you hear me?

Close your eyes.

Open your eyes.

Look left. Look right.

Without moving your head, look up. Look down.

Blink five times. (I could hear my eyelids creak like hinges.)

Clench your jaw.

Hum.

Flex your feet.

Breathe in. Hold it. Breathe out. Ok, goodnight.

I fell asleep in four minutes. I dreamed I was in a plywood-lined elevator that got stuck oscillating between the twenty-third and twenty-seventh floors until I pulled the stop lever and went plummeting, down, down into an echoey atrium where the elevator car careened into glass walls and sent me, hands outstretched, through open doors into open water. There I swam, electrified by the wires in my hands and the water, naked with an old high school friend, gazed upon by other high school friends, less mortified than I should have been, less mortified than I was when I woke up, ten and a half hours later, to a blinds-drawn sunlight and voice through the intercom: Ma'am, are you awake?

Stay where you are, I'll be right in, the voice said. Five minutes later, a woman knocked as she was opening the door and asked how I slept—better than normal? I don't recall her face but I do remember it was vastly older than the face on the ID around her neck: A football pin obscured the word "hospitals," and below smiled a young woman with bangs. Did she spend all her mornings greeting people? Did she tuck them in at night too?

I told her I slept ok, not as well as normal, that yes, I'd had dreams, that no, I don't think I woke during the night. She said I'd be taking my first nap in two hours, and until then I could do whatever I wanted besides have caffeine or medication. I wanted both, but to prove I needed stimulants to stay awake, I first had to go without. Thus, two weeks before the study and its wires, I'd stopped taking all my medication. The doctor warned me at least three times that there would be a drug test and if I failed, the whole thing would be for naught. At first I abstained from weed too but it was grad school summer break and the cicadas were loud and what else to do besides sit outside with friends, stoned? Finally I stopped, because smoking made me so excruciatingly tired that the only force that could carry me to bed was the frantic worry of not making it home before sleep hit. I often ran that last block to my house; I knew how small the window of time was before I'd be unable to move through air that thickened like setting cement.

I dazzled myself with tiredness on the second day off stimulants but denied the dazzling, saw no sparkle in the way mornings could induce sleep as much as afternoons. At my summer job in a sandwich shop, I drank as much water as possible so I could go to the fluorescent-drenched bathroom and sit down and rest. There, I'd verify being awake by verifying the terror, the levels of dread of not being asleep. I'd muster the energy to stand back up by finding a sliver of belief that the sleep study would be worth it, that numbers could be replicated even if context couldn't. Still, I was dubious of the data even before they were tallied.

Five days off stimulants, I walked to the grocery store a mile from my house. Do you need to know how I sweated?—beaded over in pixels of sweat like an enlarged comic-book character, some superhero of repose. Each step felt laced to the sidewalk, and each next step seemed not just out of reach but unimaginable. This is how walking became unfathomable. This is how I realized the stroll to the store was a mistake in both practice and intent.

I considered calling for help. I could call a friend and ask for a ride. I could wait sitting down, ease the weight of my legs, a fractional solution but a solution nevertheless. I had recently read how narcolepsy affects the appetite, now transformed into something ravenous, and lengthens the sense of distance. A ball of mozzarella in my tote bag slapped at my hip. I wished for a Pythagorean shortcut but did not call a friend.

My mom texted later that day and asked, Can't you just ignore the sleepiness? I knew she meant well. But I still said, No, at this point long past the well-being of wakefulness. I told her the tiredness felt "complete."

A woman peeled the pads from my legs, leaving ovals of fuzz-covered adhesive. The pads measured leg movements, which could suggest that restlessness was keeping me up and therefore causing my sleepiness during the day. This new doctor seemed to suspect that something along those lines was making me tired. That kind of explanation could be logical and more satisfying, but I doubted it. I knew I mostly slept through the night every night, I knew I often woke in the same position I fell asleep in, sheets still tucked tightly in, hospital corners intact. I could even sleep after drinking espresso—and in fact did, especially during the half year I lived in Barcelona, where I developed a four-espresso-a-day habit that turned into a six-a-day one until it was time to move back to the United States, where espresso is more expensive and less delicious, and where the habit, as is often the case, started to seem like a problem. Nevertheless, I bought a cheap espresso machine, packed it full of grounds a couple times a day, and slept long and often all the while. Then I quit, the first and only time.

The eye pads measured eye movements to pinpoint when I was in dream sleep. The tube under my nose measured breathing to check for sleep apnea, a disorder in which a person stops breathing for seconds or minutes at a time. It's a not-uncommon ailment.

A year after my sleep study, in the convention hall of the annual Associated Professional Sleep Societies conference, I found rows and rows of sleep-apnea contraptions—masks and tubes and nasal strips, machines that loomed like old pipey vacuum cleaners, as if the problem were a dustball to be sucked up and thrown away. I saw solutions to restless legs syndrome and shift-work disorder. At a giant booth in the middle—with its own extra-plush carpet, a tray of freshly baked cookies on the table, the oven just behind it—lay Xyrem, a.k.a. GHB, a.k.a. the date-rape drug. How it works is mysterious, but it seems to prevent attacks of sleepiness and cataplexy during the day. It's meant, medicinally and illicitly, to knock someone out. So the company that makes Xyrem adds a foul-tasting liquid and enrolls the patient in what was once called the "Xyrem Success Program." Side effects include nausea and peeing in the bed.

I first took Xyrem during a winter break from college; I wanted my parents to be there in case something went wrong. My mom watched me prepare the night's doses: I poured the liquid into two measuring cups that looked like pill bottles and topped both with water. I downed the first dose like a vodka shot, grimaced as after a vodka shot too, got in bed, and waited. I fell asleep fast, as I usually do, slept a dreamless sleep until my alarm went off four hours later, time for the second dose. Another shot thrown back, another grimace, and back into sleeping, this time into the vivid-nightmare-strewn territory that usually dominates my unconscious hours. In the morning I could taste the drug on my retainers, maybe, or maybe I just wanted to taste it to ensure it had really happened—I'd voluntarily taken a date-rape drug, twice. The lack of control while under its effects seemed sickeningly fitting, as if the only way to treat a disorder is with more disorder, entropy against entropy, all control wrested from the patient's hands and given over to pharmaceuticals that tempt with the sweet waft of warm chocolate chip cookies.

At the convention I passed by booths in search of product demos, less interested in the sales pitches directed at doctors than in the actual sensations: This is what it's like to have your nostrils pried open and this is what it's like to wear light-emitting glasses—because how the treatment feels is often as much a part of the overall experience of a disorder as is the disorder itself.

For instance, one way to treat restless legs is by attaching electrodes to them. These pulse the muscles into action, skin twitching above twitching innards, legs tired out by a machine, without any sheet-untucking jiggling.

But do restless legs even exist? And why do they arrive alongside sleep? Sometimes I think it's a syndrome invented to sell drugs and devices, but then I remind myself there are people who think the same about narcolepsy—that it's made-up, women's hysteria, sleepiness diagnosed as disorder to assuage the willpower-related worries of the so-called patient. How accurately can we gauge these subjective complaints?

The answer is sleep studies.

First there was Nyx, the goddess of night, then there were her twin sons, Thanatos, god of death, and Hypnos, god of sleep. Aristotle thought food fumes traveled to the brain and then cooled it when they sank back into the rest of the body, prompting sleep and centuries of minds emptied at night. In the eighteen hundreds, Luigi Rolando removed birds' cerebral hemispheres and watched the birds fall prey to somnolence. Scientists suggested sleep was a purging of toxic buildup. They assumed that nerves stopped communicating at night. Others wondered if time itself was being purged. Constantin von Economo sliced into the brains of dead people, probing for areas of sleep. Doctors in the 1930s placed electrodes on humans' scalps; these first modern EEGs measured the brain's electricity at night, forcing sleep to separate from waking with voltage, and making sleep studies possible.

Still, a problem remained: How can you tell just how sleepy someone is? In 1975, Mary Carskadon and William Dement created the precursor to the solution. They called it the "90-minute day." Five undergraduate students participated in the experiment, held at the Stanford University Sleep Laboratory. Their normal cycles were fractured: thirty minutes in the dark, trying to sleep, sixty minutes in the light, trying to stay awake. The schedule tricked the subjects into dreaming faster than usual.

Now, in contemporary sleep studies, patients have fewer naps but the same general pattern of a day divided by sleep. From the studies doctors draw brain waves, peaks jutting from valleys like in a skyline silhouette. In these hypnograms, the sleep monolith breaks and reveals its stages, including REM, when what's supposed to happen is so much and nothing at once—eyes moving as if awake but the body still, paralyzed to stop it from acting out dream-stories. Hence the alternate name, "paradoxical sleep."

Something was wrong in the way I created that paradox. I only looked like I slept well. Really, I slept incorrectly—in the wrong stages, at the wrong times, and never in any sort of restful way. This is narcolepsy—from *narke*, "numbness, stupor," and *lepsis*, "to seize or grasp, to take hold of." My new doctor thought this might not be the correct diagnosis. Instead, I might have idiopathic hypersomnia—the first word from *idio*, "own, personal and distinct," and *pathos*, "suffering," and the second word from the "too much" of *hyper* and the "sleep" of *somnia*. Or, as it's now understood, "unexplained and excessive sleepiness." The point of this study was to choose between the two. Or to rule one out, to cement the thing that wasn't and put in its place a diagnosis of uncertainty, a name that's more a lack than anything else, a name that's the equivalent of throwing up your hands at the problem and walking away. The ruling out could be endless. And though I worried the results would be the same as before—"the patient's complaint of excessive daytime sleepiness is not adequately explained by the parameters measured here"—I still had to go through the ceremony of naming. I still had to pretend that it didn't matter whether the sleep-study room looked like a hotel or not.

In the sleep lab I let myself become an object. Alongside wires my hair sprouted in a mess of stringy strands. I didn't wash my face when I woke so as not to upset the electrodes on my chin and temples. Why even get dressed only to sleep again? And so I sat in pajamas and a fleece, sat on the vinyl chair and on the vinyl bed, sat among objects, all of them spill-proof—all of them but me, that is, an "I" spilling data or melting into them like snow in the sudden sun of noon.

For the daytime portion of the study, I'd take five twenty-minute naps, spaced two hours apart. After every nap, awoken by a voice on the intercom telling me it had been twenty minutes, I lie-babbled like a person pretending she wasn't asleep by picking up the conversation where she left off. The problem was I hadn't left off anywhere; there was no context. There was only the void of meaning imposed by off-white sheets and off-white tables in an off-white room.

The voice would wake me, and the voice would ask if I had slept and if I had dreamed. Every time the answer to both was yes. But the data would show I hadn't actually entered REM sleep. Why were they testing me? All the questions I'd been asked from the get-go had an air of aggression to them. Had I done something suspicious? Had I mispronounced the name of a drug? I wanted answers as much as they putatively did, so why would I taint the data?

Anyway, altering the body's data would be tough no matter how much I worried about accidentally tainting it with worry. The body was the source of my measurement; I had to let the body be. But as I gave myself over to the test, I grew suspicious of my own feelings: When should I trust how I feel, and when should I trust how the measurements say I feel? If they're not the same, what's wrong, the measurements or my feelings? The sleep study results dictated a certain set of symptoms, and if I didn't actually experience those symptoms, then something wasn't right. Logic dictated it must be the measurements: When shown the test results, I'd find that they didn't match the previous two studies. Nor did they match my life. But they are correct, the doctor would say, because we followed the protocol exactly. What was I doing wrong? I'd ask. I would blame myself, I would find in the gaps between sleep-study versions the fallibility of measurement, the problem of trying to turn subjective experience objective with numbers. But those gaps would shrink with time as I convinced myself I was wrong: The numbers must be right because they're numbers, because they're without interpretation and therefore without the uncertainty caused by bias, environment, and self-reflection. I was those numbers, and no more. But without interpretation, could those numbers mean much, if anything at all?

Finally, the last nap, which went like all the other naps: asleep in three or four minutes; stage 1 sleep the whole time but a sleep still full of dreams, dreams of school rooms too small to sit in, of an accidental gun purchase, of parents cloned and turned evil, of playing a 4/4 beat on the drums; sleeves bunched up when I woke, *Infinite Jest* on the bed next to me; a cleared-throat alarm clock through the intercom that, like me, turned mechanical by the separation of sound and body—her body, her voice; my body, my data.

Then body and voice came together and the woman was in my room a quick knock later. How'd you sleep? she asked.

Just fine, I said.

Good, she said, and began peeling away the rest of my electrodes, easing them out of their glue beds, out of my hair—her fingers broad but delicate. Some women like to wash their hair twice, she said, and I wondered about those women who didn't, and all the men.

When I got home, I washed my hair twice, and like some women, I put a small dollop of cream in it for smoothing. Yes, I could be relative to other people, not just to myself. Or I could tell myself I might be. Really, I was alone—alone taking my first pill in two weeks, alone waiting for my data to arrive and to tell me whether I'd changed over those in-between-studies years, because for measurements to change, the source must too. Otherwise, how can we ever trust numbers in the first place? And there, alone, I hoped desperately that I'd stayed exactly the same, because even a solid diagnosis can make measurements worthwhile and trustworthy, can make them suggest something within gone wrong. But the lack of a name, or a name that stands in for a lack, would mean I was somehow incapable of producing meaningful measurements. What's the point of data if they don't provide certainty, if they don't stabilize? It wasn't, in fact, better to rule something out. I wanted the numbers to say "narcolepsy," because narcolepsy came from somewhere. Narcolepsy was the result of specific data. Narcolepsy was meaning. Idiopathic hypersomnia wasn't even recognized by my word-processing program. It was a failure of quantification—measurement's inability to verify or to repeat—and if what ailed me was uncertain and unverifiable, and if what ailed me came from numbers I produced, then I was uncertain and unverifiable too.

Waiting for my hair to dry, I stared at myself in the mirror.

My dress' defined waist and back zipper made me feel like I'd accomplished something. But had I? I stared a little more, let my gaze grow unfocused as the sun setting cut a last triangle of light across my mirror. Had I?

MANUAL

The word *nootropic* comes from the Greek for "mind" and "turning." To turn the mind—to move it over itself, like turning over an engine, spinning the parts alive—is to look inward. Or it is at least to believe that the solution comes from within, not from those around us. What solution? The specifics don't matter; what matters is that there is a solution—something being done—that creates the problem: not being productive or efficient enough. To solve this problem, which is less a personal problem and more a symptom of society, we might try to work with others, all those workers we're networked to; we might try to change daily demands, not to make them easier, necessarily, but to change value from quantitative to qualitative. Or we might try a nootropic, an individual, personal solution to a collective unease with the way things are.

To take a nootropic (pills called Alpha Brain or Sprint or Ciltep) is to separate oneself from the world in order to stand out in it. To take a nootropic is to demand measurement: We measure ourselves so we can compare who we are now not with other people but with previous and future versions of ourselves. Improvement, then, via nootropics and the like, becomes a necessarily solitary pursuit, with each person using the tools of the internet—apps, trackers,

&c.—to keep herself separate from the rest of the internet. To take a nootropic is to insist on the self, alone and lonely, as the source of and solution to the problems of the day.

INSTRUCTIONS

1. Feel inadequate. Feel that you're not getting enough done. Feel that other people have pulled themselves up by their bootstraps when you're still in your socks.

2. Go online to choose a collection of drugs—a "stack," in nootropics parlance—that appeals to the dual responsibility to be productive and to be independently so.

3. Wait for the shipment to arrive, tracking it obsessively in between visits to Facebook and pings from an app that asks, "What are you doing right now?"

4. Collect two days' worth of work and one day to do it.

5. Set your app to quiz you at two-hour intervals, frequent enough to collect sufficient data, infrequent enough for your productivity to thrive.

6. Take a pill. Sit down at your computer.

7. Wait for the pill to kick in, to tickle the brain into action. Feel neurotransmitter activity increasing and decreasing according to

the manufacturer's promises, because if there is no change, then what you're doing—taking a pill—is a waste of time and effort; it's inefficient.

8. Start typing. Start annotating the pill with PowerPoint slides and Excel spreadsheets. Thank Microsoft, thank the nootropics manufacturer, thank yourself.

9. Don't talk to other people—they may get in the way of your optimized state. If you must talk, listen to yourself: Hear your words flowing as they do for a nootropics-juiced Joe Rogan.

10. Track your output. Later, you can use these numbers as further justification for the pill. You can remind yourself, in moments of weakness, that it was not other people who got you to that "heightened state"—it was you (and some chemicals).

11. Go online to prove how focused you are.

12. Sign off. You don't need other people to give context to your efficiency; you already have context: what you were before the nootropics kicked in, what you will become when the nootropics wear off.

ELLIPTICAL

That lady is ripped! a dude says to his friend as I stream by on my bike. That lady is ripped, I repeat in my head—that lady is me. Freewheel whirring in downhill coast, wind against my arms during one of the last sleeveless days of fall, I arc toward the gym, its rows and rows of machines aligned by muscle and routine, that need to do something because it's what you've always done— tie the shoes the same way, use the same locker, start on the same machine—that is the heart of the gym ritual.

Walking through the locker room to the locker room door, I tighten my ripped tricep next to the mirror, glance sideways to catch the curve of muscle and then relax as I continue past the woman drying her hair under a hand dryer; the woman sitting naked in front of a mirror, putting on eyeliner; the swimmer dripping her way from pool to shower.

Just outside the door gleam two vending machines: one filled with candy, the other with soda on one half and on the other Gatorade. The drink is supposed to replace what's lost in sweat, but at the gym, the drink of choice isn't a replacement but a supplement: protein shakes, grainy greenish-brown sludge men drink from glorified sippy cups they jiggle up and down in between reps.

I walk to the second of three floors, as I always do, to do what

I do every time I go to the gym: lift weights, and before that, use the elliptical for twenty-five minutes. Or is it go on the elliptical? Or run on? Word choice depends on the relationship with the machine, whether you consider it to have pedals or paddles or platforms, whether you can pretend that the deliberate forward thrusts, which actually keep you in place distancewise, bear any resemblance to jogging (when really that resemblance is already owned by the treadmill).

A personal trainer on the stairs tells the couple trailing him that keeping a notebook is key—it's for your own personal knowledge, he says, and so you can add more reps. Without those base numbers, from where does one improve? To what does one add on? The relativity of the gym demands careful record-keeping, a supposedly objective take on reality that winnows down the subject into numerals in the name of progress: Let go of identity for the sake of the body and its mechanized system of levers and pulleys and other simple machines mirrored in the gym equipment.

The couple follows the trainer downstairs, the bro floor with no cardio machines, only racks of weights and men in T-shirts that have the sleeves cut off to draw pecs into sharp relief against bright billowing cotton. The trainer keeps turning to make sure the pair is still behind him.

A man on the other side of the stairs pulls at his shorts.

Another man plugs his headphones into his phone, the cord running up his shirt, pressed between synthetic fabric and sweat-slicked skin.

A woman pulls at her leggings.

Split into frames by glass panels, exercisers duplicate in mirrors and grow to a mass, to a metal-on-metal ringing. They hold their bodies relative to the others and compare. They keep this comparison secret but will copy movements the next day, spaced by time. The main thing is to grimace: Lips touch so sweat doesn't get in the mouth, and sweat pools above the top lip until there's too much and the drip drips from lips to rubber floor. The rubber floor absorbs the hit of barbells and says oomph at the end of a set when men cannot bear to hold on to the weights long enough to place them on the floor and so just let them go.

This is the privilege of leisure time.

A map of this place could be points of avoidance: where I stop walking toward the same machine as the man in the paisley bandanna headband because I notice his water bottle holding his spot; where I wait for someone to finish on the tricep pull-down machine, rope taut in his callused hands, and practice the look of not waiting. Some knees part away from each other and others are held apart by thighs like trunks, which is to say developed.

The gym's windows were made to hold the bodies out of reach but to hold them nevertheless. I try not to look too long. I let the rubber bear the breathing and the illusion of progress. I try to steer my attention toward the future body, more beautiful and more a specimen than the current version. But really I just want to stay the same. Sometimes the click of tendons on shoulder blades is enough.

A laminated paper sign at the top of the stairs announces the arrival of "gym wipes": Once there were black terry-cloth towels and now there are disposable alcohol-coated paper towels in a dispenser that doesn't have quite enough tension to let the perforations break. We never meant for the towels to be used for sweat on the body, the signs say.

Sometimes someone above walks by in dots, a body turned

low-res by the hole-punched metal wall. Each ass-out squat of the man squatting puts the man on the verge of losing control, his body lurching against itself like a trembling outboard motor, starting cord tugged successfully, smoke thinning over the lake.

Modern fitness comes from desk jobs and disco and heart health and dieting. It comes too, before that, from photography and war. Magazines at the turn of the twentieth century popularized the image of the superhuman strongman, with his thick neck and gladiator sandals and barrel chest. Then came wars, then the Cold War, when American presidents fretted about "soft," feminine American men. Eisenhower established the President's Council on Youth Fitness in 1956. Four years later, Kennedy wrote in *Sports Illustrated* that "the magnitude of our dangers makes the physical fitness of our citizens a matter of increasing importance." Ever since, US presidents have worried about an unfit citizenry, testing kids in school to make sure that they hit benchmarks and, it seems, based on the lack of progress, to validate these presidents' worries.

Meanwhile, Americans took to fitness on their own. Less often at the factory, more often at desks, workers with leisure time noticed their suited bodies turning mushy. Fitness could give powerful men the bodies of powerful men, and, the corporate thinking went, it could actually make them more powerful. Exercising, and having the world know you exercise, became morally virtuous. If you could control nothing else in your life, at least you could control your body. People performed health in the private public of gyms, turning it into an individual pursuit, with proof of each person's willingness to give over leisure time to self-improvement evident in the most public of spaces: the body. The gym was the factory and in it, machines, like the machines of regular factories, replicated human movements. But in these new factories, the workers were the product and the consumer at once.

I never like to admit I use the elliptical. It's a women's machine, I'm told, both explicitly and by all the women on all the ellipticals, hair flopping in sync with the beaten cyclical orbits that move less like Earth's and more like Pluto's. Per the standard thinking, because women use ellipticals more than men do, ellipticals are considered lesser—less real, maybe, or just less difficult. The number of calories burned, according to the elliptical (an estimate at best, like all machines', but a number nevertheless), suggests otherwise. The movement does too: Each step comes with a punch forward, a pull back, arms connected to poles connected to foot paddles, a bad bow-and-arrow imitation. The heels gently tap in the downswing, the legs like tongs.

Lines of ellipticals, lines of treadmills, bicycles, stair climbers, each front row prime real estate because it faces the windows—the windows the street, its gray cracked concrete that makes every car sound like it has a flat tire—and not the hamstrings and calves of the going-nowhere orbiters in front. The word "machine" is anathema to the idea of these machines; they are supposed to reproduce the natural, real activity so closely—some of the bicycles even have videogame courses that require steering and gear shifting—that users won't notice they're not going anywhere. On the treadmill, there is everything but forward motion and the task of passing other people on the sidewalk, deciding whether to weave right or left around another body, steps softening, momentarily, so as not to alarm anyone. On the stair climbers there are real stairs. On every machine, including the bastard elliptical, what's replicated most closely, though, is yesterday's stint on the same machine. Motivation turns muddy: If you're not at the gym because you can't be outside, moving in the real world, then why are you there?

On my way to the elliptical in the front left corner, five machines from the nearest exerciser, I see someone I know and consider exit strategies: the opposite direction, toward the upper deck of the pool, around the staircase, down the staircase, toward the stationary bikes, darting toward the weights and skipping the elliptical altogether—which I try for, but she does too, sees me, asks, What's up? and I point to my iPod clipped to my T-shirt hem and mumble some nonsense, after pretending I hadn't yet noticed her, about being in a Beyoncé zone. She smiles, as eager to end the conversation as I, zigzags past me, waves goodbye as she bounds down the steps, away.

Around me, around the elliptical I muscle into motion, drops of sweat gather on the floor, as if the rubber itself were perspiring. I can't hear myself breathe over my music playing through noise-canceling headphones except when the seal between ear canal and earbud cracks open, loosened by moisture. I notice slowly, mostly by feel, then by sound: the creak of the machine every time my right foot comes forward, my breath on the downbeat, the foot-on-plastic of the overzealous runner who kicks the hollow front of the treadmill on each gazelle spring into the same place.

As exercisers multiplied, so did gyms and so did equipment: To barbells and dumbbells were added weightlifting machines, which narrowed each exercise down into a simple movement, the bench press becoming a seated push forward, the squat becoming recliner-based. By connecting the lifter to the weights with cables, and by seating the lifter in an apparatus that allowed only specific movements, a machine could keep the body controlled. It could hold the body in place. It was the modern gym itself, writ small.

Machines for cardiovascular exercise popped up too, bringing running indoors, to the treadmill, on which distance and time were complemented with new metrics: calories, METs, watts—metrics that grew more arbitrary the more of them there were.

Next came fitness classes. People lined up in rows and columns like aerobics machines, faced mirrors instead of windows, and formed, willingly, into a panopticon. At the spinning classes I used to go to, at six thirty in the morning, often I was one of only two or three participants. As the teacher barked commands and encouragement—Climb that hill! Come on, y'all!—I tried to ignore the room's emptiness, the bass soaked up by just a few bodies, the bass that bounced off the hard walls and buzzed with the flicker of fluorescent lights beyond the door, the bass that beat against the sea of black light in the cycling studio that turned our bodies into rickety jellyfish. White towels draped on our handlebars gleamed in artificial brilliance.

I liked to choose a bike about three-quarters of the way back, on the side closest to the door. I'd stand next to the bike, lower the saddle until it was even with my hipbone, and turn the screeching bolt until nothing wobbled. The class always began with a "cadence check": We'd spin our pedals into a chain-driven hum, adjusting resistance until we were moving without much effort at a certain number of revolutions per minute. Difficulty was relative to ability: There were no numbers on the bright red dials we turned to tighten or loosen the hold on the bike's flywheel, only the feeling of the effort of spinning in place. Knowing yourself, per the quantified-self fantasy of knowledge through numbers, was as simple as listening to the teacher say, Eighty rotations a minute, please. All other variables, unnumbered, fell away. Gears didn't matter, no one could pull ahead, no one could fall behind, and we all sweated together but individually, each moving according to personal tolerance for discomfort, or for "pushing yourself," depending on your take on willpower: Is it the willingness to bear a burden, or is it the drive to succeed?

In the gym, it's both. There is no endpoint. Once, after getting home from the gym and showering, while standing at the bathroom sink putting on mascara, five minutes to spare before leaving for work, a subway ride underwater during which I could have put on mascara like other women, entire polka-dotted makeup bags spilled out on their laps, I realized I would be standing there putting on mascara every morning forever with five or ten minutes to spare, a subway ride ahead or not—I would be doing this for the rest of my life. And when a clump glued together my eyelashes, and a piece of black flaked onto my cheek, I realized too that not only would I be doing this same thing forever, I'd be doing it imperfectly forever. Every morning a new mistake. Or every morning, more optimistically, a chance for improvement.

And so I found myself a few days later, walking back from the gym, about a half hour before daily mascara application, walking so automatically that I couldn't even remember leaving the gym, trudging down its sticky indoor stairway and out onto the street, where bodegas offered ATMs and beer and the only people outside had dogs, that trudging the trudging of physical exhaustion early in the morning but also the trudging of daily repetition. Every day some kind of fitness—in the winter, indoors, the same walk there and back, a collection of similar exercises only occasionally shifted upward a notch, in more reps or weight. The improvements were for improvement's sake—so I could see the numbers rising—a way to distinguish now from before, before from the future, when things would be the same and different because, while each machine moves only one way, there's always a whole stack of weights waiting to be pinned to the cable.

Prancing on the elliptical, I happen to glance up from my magazine propped atop the machine, covering the nagging timer, to see the man on the ElliptiGO heading east in the right-hand lane of a six-lane street. Every day I spot him through the second-story window. The bright green tubes of the thing—a bicycle-like device driven by an elliptical movement, rather than by regular pedaling—catch my peripheral vision. I see him and I scoff. Why not ride a bike? He's doing it backward: Instead of making the real-life transportation stationary and stabilizing in the gym, he's turned an exercise machine into a vehicle, deliberately shedding the control the gym offers. He has a single metric—distance—to measure his progress, and he has the entire real world around him, not exercising, distracting from his pursuit of himself.

When his whole body lunges forward it actually does, whereas above, in the steel and glass of the gym, I lunge to stay in place, each push forward the backswing for the next but also a rewinding of movement, like each next step is a redo of the last. His progress is too literal.

From my stationary machine, I watch him imitate me, and I see in the window's dim reflection me imitating him, and in this doubling I grow dizzy, which the machine warns in a very serious serif typeface is a sign I should stop exercising and see a doctor, rest until I can see straight, but I won't stop and wait to climb back on because I've already climbed on, I'm already watching the man on the ElliptiGO and between us window washers on a crane one floor below, where they're scrubbing away the film that gives me myself, bounced back in makeshift mirror, and in removing that film removing the veil between my leisure time working out and the non-leisure time of the workers outside, but only temporarily, because later it will rain and pollen and the dust from the construction site across the street will dry on the window, turning it opaque enough to hold me again and in that holding force me, because habit is repetition is habit, to come back the next day to verify I can still do exactly what I did the day before.

EARLY

T he clocks were set to central daylight time on the day I was born. The clock on the microwave next to the stove where my dad was boiling water for pasta read four and some minutes when, from the living room, my mom said, I think we need to go to the hospital. She and my dad got in the car with no bags, none of the Sunday newspapers they'd spent the afternoon reading, and drove east toward Lake Shore Drive, which they'd take south to Michael Reese Hospital.

There are seven clocks in my one-bedroom apartment, two that tick loudly, two that don't tick, and three digital ones, all set to slightly different times not on purpose but because achieving such widespread accuracy is tough when you're twisting hands on faces with no numbers and constantly resetting the one digital clock that runs slow because it's meant to be connected to DC power.

I was born on Memorial Day weekend, a Sunday. Chicago was clear and warm, perfect for barbecues.

I started wearing a watch as soon as I could tell time. My first watch's hands had tiny blue faces and names and a story from Swatch: Flik goes quick and Flak stays back. More than two decades later, I worry about time both near and far: how long it'll take me to walk to my afternoon meeting, how long it'll take me to fall in love with a yet-unmet man, how long it'll be before I and this man who doesn't exist get married. Every time another friend posts a photo on Facebook with her fiancé, her hand on his shoulder so you can see the diamond in iPhone flash, the panic bubbles. My current boyfriend, whom I don't suspect I'll marry, tells me I misuse "jealousy" and "envy."

Sun fell through the windows of the maroon Volkswagen Golf onto my mom, reclined as far as her seat would allow. She was upright enough to see, just before the entrance to the Drive, that traffic was nearly stopped until at least Navy Pier, and upright enough to also see, in the sideview mirror, a canine-unit police cruiser a few cars away. My dad got out to talk to the police. My wife is in labor, he said to the canine-unit man. Follow me closely, the man said. They weaved through the dense traffic all the way south, where they exited, headed briefly west, and reached the hospital, two months early. My mom found the nearest wheelchair and sat in it.

If being late is a sign of self-involvement, then being early should be a sign of selflessness. But it's not. It too is a kind of self-involvement, a deliberate refusal to measure accurately—and show up on time—because of the egotistical notion that your presence—you being somewhere—is so important that it's best to err on the side of early.

I used to set my watches early, not to trick myself into being on time, as the chronically late may do, but to have the feeling, any time I looked at my wrist, that I was already early.

Taped in my dad's baby book are a lock of brown hair, the first tooth he lost. In it are Wisconsin-cursive lists of birthday presents and friends and milestones: walking, talking, adding, bike-riding—each with a date, and every year with a set of height and weight numbers, an upward trajectory that ended at thirteen years old. How much can time hold? How much can data tell us? I do not know how large thirteen-year-old boys should be, so my dad's 63 inches and 103 pounds are unremarkable—or, rather, remarkable not for their content but for their specificity, for the fact that they exist at all.

In the hospital my mom told the nurse she hadn't yet gone to Lamaze classes, she didn't know what she was doing. The nurse told her to pick something physical to focus her gaze on, so my mom looked out the sixth-floor east-facing window and found in the turquoise wide-waled lake a sailboat to stare at. But then it was late-spring evening, and the sailboat disappeared into the reflective black of night over water, and there was no more looking and there was no more waiting: I was born.

So began my fraught relationship with the clock, that device to set and measure against, to check and deny and obsess over, that metaphor for money so weakly stripped of its nonfigurative roots. Always afraid of being late, I started young being early—to the school bus stop right in front of my house, to turn in homework and dotted-line handwriting exercises in kindergarten, where my teacher suggested I would have more luck closing the space between the spine of the lowercase *h* and its hump if I stopped rushing. But I couldn't: There was always time to run out of, and the space remained.

I didn't cry at first. Why isn't she making any noise? my mom asked. No one answered. They whisked me away. It wasn't until the next morning that they let my mom hold me.

My mom holds my anxieties: You will have enough time to get everything done, she says, because you always do. Have you ever turned something in late? she asks, and I don't have to tell her no—all I have to do is look down in defeat, beaten again by my own habits.

From the start I was measured in time: born two months early, crying five minutes late.

In elementary school, being late was called being tardy. You could rack up tardies. Or you could have a pathological problem with the risk of being on time, not even tardy, and dash out the door each morning with the weight of worry in your mouth, and every morning, you, which is to say I, could and would tell my dad, who walked me to school, that it was his fault we were going to be late, only to tell him, when we rounded the last corner and saw the black asphalt and backstop and the tan brick school building I wouldn't need to be in for another fifteen minutes, that I was sorry, only to do it all again the next day.

Time segments, time builds up.

If being early is being ahead of time, then being early is dwelling in emptiness.

At the airport my dad always used to a buy a newspaper or go to the bathroom right as the plane was about to board. My mom would get upset. I learned to imitate her, and then I learned to be upset on my own. But I didn't learn to get as nervous at airports as she does. I'm comfortable with an hour buffer: enough time to wait in unexpectedly long lines and still get a snack but not so much time that my butt will go numb from sitting on hard terminal chairs. The one time I almost missed a flight, I got to the gate as people were boarding. I'd convinced the TSA agents to let me cut to the front of the security line only to have my bag searched by hand. They'd found the weathered brick, harvested from my parents' backyard, that I intended to use as a bookend. We can't let you bring this on, the man told me. I know you wouldn't, but you could hit someone with it, he explained. Maybe I wanted to check it? No, I said, I do not want to check my brick—you can keep it. He placed it in a bin below the conveyor belt, and I dashed off to my gate, weaving around rolled suitcases and beeping electric carts, very on time if the place weren't an airport, where an on-time passenger is considered late and an on-time flight is considered early.

Outside a bar in Barcelona, a man asked my friends and me if any of us had a lighter. We were standing in a circle under a cloud of smoke that rose to a curlicued metal balcony above. A friend handed over a red Bic. The man said thanks, asked if we had the time, and we all turned to each other as he cupped his hand around his cigarette; I could hear his lips against the filter. Eventually the gazes fell on me, the only one with a watch. I thrust my wrist forward and showed him the round white face, unwilling to attempt the math: In

Catalan, time is a matter of addition and subtraction. If it's 1:34, it's two quarters of two, plus four. Time crumbles and builds around convenient numbers, those upright-minute-hand times on which we agree to meet because they seem less arbitrary than the numbers not divisible by five or ten. Catalan time hovers around itself, as if focusing, the calculations drawing nearer to the exact number, dancing like moths aiming for the light. Telling time in Catalan is like telling time with a watch purposely set wrong: You set it that way because you think the math will be too cumbersome and the purposely wrong time will have its intended effect; you stop looking at clocks in Barcelona, hoping you can live with the relaxed attitude of a place where dinner doesn't happen till long after the sun has set and the banks close at lunchtime. But the math becomes easier, then it becomes a habit, and the time of everything shifts but remains time, which is, if anything, exact.

If I know I'll always be early, then why don't I always leave late?

The future has an end.

A friend and I have been wondering about the passage of time and tall buildings: Does time pass more slowly or more quickly for a person on the top floor? We keep not looking up the answer online. We trace orbits through the air between us with both hands, our elbows the center points around which planets spin.

Lately I've been waking up early, by which I mean before my alarm. The red minutes taunt me, pale against the easing morning. I'm either afraid I won't wake up when it goes off or I'm operating according to a slightly faulty internal clock, one so programmed by years of punctuality-induced anxiety it won't let even the start of the day arrive on time. When I do make it till the alarm, I'm pleased: I'm not impatient for the day to start, but I'm impatient for the night to end. Or I'm impatient to get the next thing started, because the next thing is often all I think about.

Time zones were standardized for railroads. Without common clocks, distance would strand people in time and send trains crashing into one another. Now, getting to the train early means shivering under the heat lamps or shivering in the dripping tunnel, men around me I don't trust, space to maintain.

If I don't get married in the next year, then my clock will diverge from my parents'—I won't get married at the age they did. And if I don't get married in the next year, then what. Then I'll fantasize even more about time travel, even more about men, about being younger so the deadline is further away, so the ticking time can keep ticking until—

to match the story, but not all of it. Not the bedrest months, not the months of not being pregnant but wanting to be, not the dead-too-early parents. But the marriage—I wouldn't mind that.

I still have to say in my head a fake TV promo—"Eight, seven central"—to remember which way the time zones move.

At the wedding of the first of my friends to get married, standing at the front of the church in a blue bridesmaid dress and gold heels, hair in an updo that required twenty-five bobby pins, I wondered what the audience saw when they looked at me.

Yes, I realized, life goes by faster at the top of a building, like at the peak of a panic.

As a kid I'd get to school early, judo practice early, I'd finish standardized tests and reading assignments early, but I wouldn't, it turns out, finish math tests early. Sitting on a metal chair, plastic desk prone to hand-squeaking holding the stapled exam, sometimes I wouldn't finish at all. I'd be so nervous about running out of time that I'd run out of time. The sound of pencils, frantic tapped bursts and hurried erasing like fabric rubbed against itself, the four sure lines of a boxed answer like someone announcing "I got it right"—it would all hold me unwriting at that desk, facing so much unlined white paper to be filled in so little time until that time was up.

Time runs like colors, like tights. Time crawls and time passes—not away, in euphemistic death, but by, like passing by a storefront.

Now I yearn for extra time in life, that boring existential desire of a person who has the luxury of worrying about meeting self-imposed life-stage deadlines.

Why, when a friend was waiting to be picked up at the airport by two dude friends, was she not mad when they showed up forty-five minutes later than promised? Why, she asked me, did she tell them it was fine when, had the friends been women, she would've been pissed? We blame it on societal expectations, she said. That's like blaming pain on a bruise: Where did the bruise come from?

A woman needs only to say "I'm late" in a certain tone of voice to convey either fear or hope.

My computer calendar now offers to remind me of an event when I need to leave for it. But that's much too late: I might not be dressed yet, I might not have decided whether I'm going to walk or take the train. It's too late because the time at which I need to leave is already too late to leave to be early.

The night I was born, while my mom was in labor, my dad called my grandfather to ask him to take the dog out. Right after, my mom's doctor showed up, in white pants and a pastel blouse, arriving straight from a Memorial Day barbecue. She hadn't had time to change.

Because I was born early, there was, until I was eight months old, no place for me on the growth charts. I'd jumped the gun so much that I couldn't even be counted, and everyone else couldn't be my context. It was as if I existed in a vacuum in which time was absolute and I was never even early (or late) because there was no one else to show up.

Being late is needing an excuse: I was stuck on the train, the train never came, I spilled a bottle of lotion, I forgot my umbrella. The excuse can be real or fake—it matters only for the one saying it, not the excuser. The trouble comes when a real excuse was in the repository of fake ones, and the late person feels like she's wasting it when she has to use it as truth.

I was stuck at the hospital for twenty-five days. When my parents took me home, I came with a beige apnea monitor the size of a picnic basket. For three months, an alarm would sound if I stopped breathing or if the wires disconnected. Every day no alarm, the same data, and time was passing, and my parents were growing tired of the testing at home and the testing at the hospital and finally, they said, Enough.

Even then you were early, my mom told me once. She meant impatient.

My first phrase was "not a baby, a girl." Already I was defining myself in terms of time, on a timeline on which each moment of now passes inexorably from the future into the past, per Aristotle: "Whenever we notice the before and after, then we say that there is time."

My mom did not worry about me being born early. She wonders now why she didn't worry more.

It can be too early to tell, too late to make a difference. It can be too early in the morning, too late at night. It can be an early surprise or a late change, an early predictor or a late adjustment.

It can be early days, like when I first embarked on the project of being late more often. I'd sometimes succeed in showing up at the college dining hall after whomever I was meeting, but mostly I'd fail and would still get there first, ticking away time by doing the student-newspaper crossword.

My Sunday paper arrives late Saturday night, and whenever I come home to it and reach down to pick up the puckered blue bag, I like to think I'm time-traveling. But then I feel older, and I remember I'm supposed to be worried about meeting the deadlines of growing up.

For the past week my computer has been unable to open the "Time" Wikipedia page. It spends a few seconds frantically loading and reloading the site before it gives up and goes gray, telling me an error has occurred.

The only rule is time, but really the only rule is expectations.

AWAKE

nside a spansule of Adderall are tiny beads, and inside each of these is a mix of salts. These salts in spheres in capsules can make a person stay awake. They can also make the restless focused and the focused restless. They give me what I imagine to be a healthy level of alertness, and even when I fall asleep just minutes after taking one, upright on the couch or defeated back in bed, I am glad for them, because it is against this medicine that I measure possibility—of being awake, of being with other people, of being. Because of that measurement, I have something to focus on, always, something to hold my unrelated anxieties. Because of that measurement, I can be sure I'm trying to be productive, and these days, that's the best you can ask of someone, at least in public.

In the relative private of my friend's car, driving to Minneapolis along highways flanked by fields both fallow and full, I was getting tired. So I reached into the tiny pants pocket with my pointer and thumb and tweezed out my pocket pill, glanced away from the billboard-free road to look at my friend and make sure she was still reading while I instinctively swished around some spit, and dry-swallowed it. She knew I took the pills, but still, I didn't want to call attention to it, because she was a new friend, and I was trying to seem "normal," an effort I air-quoted when I thought it, as if protecting my ego from its own judgment. We were going to Minneapolis to see the Nine Inch Nails, a band I lied about liking because I was trying to make friends in the town I'd moved to a month before.

The pill wasn't enough. I knew it wouldn't be because it never is when I drive, but I still hope, every time, thinking that maybe I'll have calibrated everything well enough for the medicine to obviate the Coke Zero or iced coffee I usually drink on long drives, their caffeinated push augmented by the sleep-disabling need to pee. Inevitably, I overdo the caffeination, but it doesn't become apparent until I arrive and find myself shaking and sweaty as I unpack the car with the manic enthusiasm of someone looking for a misplaced wallet in her own house, tearing through drawers and moving every object because movement feels like a solution.

When we got to Minneapolis, I raced to get everything out of the car and into the place we were staying, the house of my friend's friends, who were out of town. As my friend punched the code into the digital front door lock, I wondered if I should ask for it, driven by the need to plan and the tendency to always expect the worst. The keys depressed and popped out one by one, each depression triggering the spring-out of the last button. Inside, trying to make my avoidance of the house's two cats seem like I was restless, not afraid of cats, I worried that I'd taken the pill too early in the day, that it wouldn't last through the concert, despite the caffeine rushing me unasleep as if through subtraction.

On the living room couch, I emptied my backpack, fishing out clothes for the night. I wondered how late the concert would go, googled on my phone any city ordinances that might give me a hint, pretended to be nonchalant when I asked my friend as we stood side by side in the bathroom, putting on makeup. Who knows, she said.

I needed to know. Taking a pill that regulates day and night makes interruptions to routine threatening. Each extra hour awake, tacked on by a delayed subway or a party that's more fun than not; or each extra hour for sleep, provided by work finished early or a friend who's canceled the evening's plans—those extra hours could be impossible. Pills mean a regimented waking, one created to take the place of sleeping rather than to complement it. Often, before going out on a Saturday night, I'll take a nap, wake, and spend the hours between the day's second waking and leaving waiting for the proper time to take the night's pill if only to adhere to a plan whose value is in its existence, not its timing.

But no matter when I end up taking the pill, I can still be asleep whenever I want. I can always sleep, stand in the collision of day and night—the flattening dusk light smearing navy and black across the remaining shadows, erasing them—and opt for the latter so easily it's like I'm opting to blink or worry: It happens because there's no way for it not to happen.

Bad seats and misogynistic lyrics aside, the concert was just fine, if not memorable. We watched the show and watched people watching the show, an endless mass of shaved-head men resembling white supremacists who greeted each other with handshake bro-hugs. We loud-whispered about people we knew. We took turns going to the bathroom. I stayed adequately awake but not alert enough to remember the smaller details of the night, perhaps because the band was made bland by the stadium or the corporatization of alternative rock, or maybe just in relation to my other thoughts, which mainly centered on this new friend and whether she liked me, a concern that was tied up in the overarching and common concern: I must not seem uptight by going to bed early.

I never know what to do with my body at concerts, and this one was no different. I jiggled my leg to the beat, aware of the effort it took to unstick my heel from the soda-stained concrete floor. On stage, lights flashed from all sides, and forty-five minutes in, a screen came down, transforming the musicians into silhouette cutouts and then, as the strobe fell into sync with the music, an industrial-rock flipbook. The bass throbbed into my ribs and, after the second encore, I turned to my new friend and asked if she wanted to leave early to beat the crowd. On the street my pummeled eardrums muffled the grinding traffic, and I talked too quietly to compensate for what I thought was shouting.

A cab brought us to a shitty pizza and tattoo parlor, where the flicker of overhead lights became clearer as I became less clear, my soggy blinking falling into the rhythm of the fluorescent bulbs, my eyes closing to this visual lullaby. Our pizza arrived, we doused it with red pepper flakes, and we left to walk the five blocks back to the Lynnhurst house where we were staying.

You must know by now that the digital door lock would be our demise, our roadblock to sleeping through the dead of night. You must know that my pills were inside the house while I was outside, yawning my way into nocturnal oblivion.

We could get into the garage though, and, convinced that there was a spare key that would materialize if we just looked hard enough, my friend began rifling through everything, opening the motorcycle's seat, picking up clay pots and running her hands along smoothly painted windowframes. You grew up with a garage, she said—Where'd you hide the extra key?

We didn't have an extra key, I said, feeling bad about my lack of insight.

Across the yard, behind the kitchen window, open just wide enough for a hand but not an arm, the cats watched, their worthless gazes taunting us with the very simple fact that they were inside and we were not.

The nearest hotels had abysmal Yelp reviews, which we read quickly because of dwindling phone batteries, then in the single digits. The only thing open nearby was 24/7 Fitness. Or so we thought. The windows were permanently steamed over, blurring the view of empty ellipticals. "24/7" was a lie—but isn't it always? Circadian rhythm, that cyclical structure for everything from cell growth to body temperature, prevents the twenty-four-hour day from being all daytime: Night happens because it must, because when the sun falls below the far edge of land and the stars trace animals across the sky, darkness puts most of the world to sleep. Except when it doesn't, as in those nocturnal anomalies, bats and email servers and night-shift workers, overstimulated bankers and students and late-night revelers, awake to prove they can be.

Stimulants don't do away with the circadian clock—they just fuck with it. The pendulum of a real clock would be wrenched aside during the stimulated hours, a simulated suspension of time, maintained by amphetamine salts. Amphetamine, part of the substance now marketed as Adderall, was first synthesized in 1887. People inhaled it for nasal congestion. Then they discovered its animating effects, and ever since, they've taken it to stay focused and awake. The pace of work quickens, and the chug of hours slows. Hearts pump with chemical zeal—hence my uncle's draft-dodging strategy of popping speed continuously for a couple of weeks before the army medical examination. His blood pressure shot up high enough to avoid the war. During that war, amphetamines were prescribed for, among other things, weight loss, while their sleep-inducing complement, sedatives, was prescribed for anxiety, itself a side effect of speed. Cycles occur naturally, even when they move artificially.

But cycles change, and the more people take stimulants, the more those who don't are pressured to, dragged into the medically restructured day in which waking grows and sleep shrinks. The body, sped into nonstop work, becomes the source of value, and for the source of value to be productive, it has to be switched on: It has to be awake.

Still in the garage, wondering what to do, I worried about missing too much sleep, as though sleep were something that could be missed, like a scene in a movie while you're talking or the bus while you're dawdling by the front door. Or I worried about being awake too long, because the flipside of lack of sleep is excess experience, abjectly tacked onto the evening, when night desaturates the sky. It makes no difference what happens during the night awake; what matters is how it feels in the morning, when the choice to sleep—the illusion of that choice—is gone, when you must be awake because society expects it, because the split of time into day and night requires adherents in order to have adherents.

Adderall adheres. When a pill turns wet it gets sticky, clings to hands or the bathroom sink it was dropped in. In the throat and stomach, it gets wetter still, dissolves into the blood and later the brain, where it increases dopamine and norepinephrine activity. On Reddit, some people report that when it hits it feels like "a strong cup of coffee"; others find it more subtle—"like going from just woke up to 12:30 in the afternoon. You don't register the change and you don't feel unnatural, but it's there." For me, it creeps up—I don't even notice it's working unless I happen to notice I'm no longer tired. More often, though, I notice only after the fact, when the fatigue creeps in, when lunch or reading or talking on the phone puts me into a stupor.

In the garage, the post-concert, post-five-hour-drive, post-big-dinner stupors all combined into one menacing exhaustion that made me panic: Locked out, no phone batteries left, we could either try to sleep in the garage or go to a fire station, where we might recharge our phones.

My friend is better with strangers than I—she has that combination of no-nonsense bluntness and a sweet, pleading smile that melts away interpersonal boundaries—so we decided she'd do the talking. We rang the bell—fire stations have doorbells!—and saw through tinted glass a man with sleep creases on his face, navy khakis and a white undershirt, shuffling to the door to let us in. None of the night-shift firemen had iPhones, but one had a clock radio with an iPod dock—maybe that would work? We followed the sleep-creased man in silence to the bedroom, my friend clicked her phone into the dock, and we continued on to the living room, where, as if waiting for us, were two recliners and an enormous TV. You can watch whatever you want, the fireman said, handing us the remote, tone of voice like a teen-movie dad. The building murmured sleep, a ticking furnace and rustling sheets, another person half-awake. Time must have passed; we'd fallen asleep, because suddenly I was blinking to the thud of a wool blanket hitting my curled body.

At some nameless hour of the morning, there was an alarm that would turn out to be false. I curled up tighter, still worried the cold would prevent me from getting a good night's rest, as if that were the only thing getting in the way. Light beamed from the hallway, and I watched through eyelashes as large men slipped lithely back and forth, donning heavy pants and jackets that thumped onto their shoulders, stepping into boots that coughed with each step against the linoleum floor. An intercom announced the address, a siren Dopplered away and lulled us, in its half arpeggio, back into the teeth-grinding, muscle-clenched sleep of a nighttime spent somewhere unfamiliar.

Many people complain of the Adderall crash: The long-acting pill begins to wear off after about seven hours. Then it settles into its half life, leaving the body quickly enough that dopamine levels plummet. The mood follows. "I'm angry and I'm a mess," writes one person on Reddit. "I didn't want to do anything or talk to anybody. I just wanted to crawl into my bed and die," writes another.

Despite the crash, the crasher may not be able to sleep. Her efficient productivity may turn to profound irritability with sudden-onset hunger and single-word speech. As the regulation ends, chaos seeps in, sleep remains just out of reach. One friend worries whether the pill was worth taking to begin with. To soothe such anxiety, this friend will go over how many pages he's written, seeking evidence that he was more productive than usual, that the pill did its job, that it wasn't wasted. He'll feel better, he says. But it won't be any easier to sleep. For that, he smokes weed.

Sometimes smoking doesn't work either, and at this point, he realizes he's failed in a different way, having timed it all wrong so the comedown comes too late. When this happens, when tiredness finally hits but night has already turned into early morning, sleep disappears.

For any of us tired at the wrong time, the solution is to regulate with medicine, overriding the natural order of activity and rest and replacing it with an artificial version. Narcoleptics are rearranged into normal sleeping and waking patterns, and healthy people enjoy productive days in which sleep is a matter of willpower. Adderall, the medical answer to a disorder, is also the solution to the disorder of a day, the uncertainty of whether you'll be alert enough to get everything done. Those who remain unmedicated—refusing to treat sleep like a symptom or illness—are like those who keep using VHS tapes and DVDs; they are living according to an outmoded, unpopular technology. Whether the new technology is better doesn't matter as long as it's prevalent. Anyone who thinks it's a shame we can't sleep according to our natural cycles may or may not be right, but she almost certainly is falling behind in the race to do more, whether it's more parties or more spreadsheets.

Despite the alarms and the uncomfortable recliners, we managed to sleep, but briefly, because soon it was seven, time for breakfast and the firefighters' shift change. I slowly regarded my watch, trying to make my movements appear like mere stretching. Before either of us could muster whatever morning confidence is necessary to wake up in a room of men, we kept our eyes closed and listened to the firemen outline the virtues of having a dog postdivorce. It's a problem coming up with something to say when you're surrounded by chatting firefighters. You pop into consciousness mid-discussion totally aware that the conversationalists have seen you in the intimate embrace of dreaming.

But it was time. After tossing each other knowing looks that suggested "We can't keep up the charade," we eased our bodies upright and craned our necks with couch-induced soreness. The firefighters nodded our way and said, Good morning. We trudged to the kitchen counter, looking spectacularly bedraggled in the blue-white light. It was only while giving us each a bottle of seltzer that they wondered: So, why are you girls here? We explained, and the one with the crew cut that had grown out the most said: Well, let's take a look at the house. Maybe we can get in because, you know, we're firefighters—we break into stuff all the time.

Why walk two blocks when a fire truck can drive you the same distance? Why close your eyes, succumbing to sleep deprivation's heavy-lidded gravity, when you can grin and watch yourself in the window of a fire truck live out a childhood dream?

Even with their help, we could not get in. There was an open window on the second floor, but the firefighters couldn't justify cutting the screen unless, they said, you've got a baby in there or something. We had no baby, so instead of breaking in, the firefighters did what you'd do for any exhausted person: They took us to Starbucks.

Just as Adderall is the poor person's cocaine, so caffeine is the drug-averse's Adderall. In coffee shops everywhere, the air beats with the ritual of collectively waking up in public. The caffeinated drink, like the speed pill, lets each person approach productivity, giving structure to the workday—a capitalism-friendly promise of pure efficiency.

As we sat wedged into the back seat of the truck, backpack strap–style seat belts over our shoulders, we smiled a little less broadly than before, the pomp of a fire truck ride overshadowed by the physical letdown of sleep deprivation. I saw past my reflection in the windows to strip-mall storefronts and trees blown half-bare by the onset of autumn.

A few hours into our Starbucks stint, we had no other option but to break in. The walk back was the longest mile, the exaggerated weight of each step, one after another in an ever-so-gradual shortening of the distance between us and that house, the open window, my medicine. I had some pills in an Altoids Smalls tin in my backpack, more in the glove box of my car, in another tin, still more in a pill bottle in the living room. They were everywhere, but they were all locked away.

The sun off the white sidewalk was sharp and bright but not strong enough to unsettle the chill that had begun setting into our bodies the night before. Eventually restaurants and parking lots and giant blocks of apartments gave way to houses and driveways and bags of leaves along the curbs.

I didn't recognize the house when we arrived. It seemed smaller. Perhaps the presence of other people scaled it down. We walked around to the back and got a ladder out of the garage, dragged it sloppily to the front of the house, and propped it against the second floor siding. While my friend held the base, I climbed to the top, each hollow step against aluminum muffled by tree branches and the birds in them. I sliced open the screen with the gardening shears I'd put in my back pocket, and wriggled in head first, letting my body flop over the windowsill like a towel heavy with water, my jeans scraping the rough-edged screen like an emery board.

My friend asked me for a pill as we were packing the car. Gone was the zeal for travel I'd had the day before, and with it, my enthusiasm for the weekend. I had lost so much sleep, and surely that didn't bode well for the days ahead.

Car key in hand, eager to get going and too eager to seem laid back and "chill" to this new friend, I said ok. We took the pills together, washing them down with the last of the fire-station seltzer, now nearly flat. She spent the car ride with her eyes locked to her iPad screen, typing nonstop on a keyboard balanced on her lap, foot tapping against the passenger-side door. I guzzled coffee, counted the miles left, and worried about falling asleep.

I'm still not sure whether I have a problem with healthy people taking other people's prescribed medications, whether because this friend was doing schoolwork I was helping her cheat. Maybe I shouldn't have handed over my medication so easily to her, because by giving it away, I turned myself into a pushover and a faker: If I really needed the pills, then I wouldn't be able to give them away, the logic goes; if I were really so tired, I'd be taking all the pills I could.

I said no the next time my friend asked, and eventually, she found another source—a coworker with a fake ADHD diagnosis— and stopped asking. She stockpiled enough pills to sell them to our friends, and when everyone had their own little stockpiles, a new tradition emerged: "Addy Friday," a day of intense typing and chain-smoking at the coffee shop down the street. When they'd ask if I wanted to join, I'd joke: Every day is Addy Friday. Though true, it still didn't make me feel any less left out. Every Friday, when the Nine Inch Nails friend nervously picked off all her nail polish and her boyfriend couldn't answer questions and his best friend couldn't eat—every Friday, we were living according to opposing game plans, they on the side of intense wakefulness, with sleep nowhere in sight, me barely wakeful, always arcing toward night.

They were like overclocked computers, machines that have been hacked to be as powerful as possible without overheating. If I wasn't working diligently enough or staying up late enough, it's because I wasn't trying as hard according to modern time standards; it's because I was behind the times.

LEAVING

t's hard not to giggle while ignoring a shirtless, sunburned man chugging beer from a headless lawn-ornament flamingo, his friends calling him "dickhead" in support, while overhearing voices from the front of the bus saying the GPS is wrong, we're lost, and while trying, from behind sunglasses, to pretend to be asleep. But so it was, as two friends and I hitched a ride to Rock Valley, Iowa, the starting line for the weeklong bike ride across the state that would begin the next day.

See? Even the angry one thinks it's funny, one of them said.

I tried not to flinch. The problem was bigger than the uneasy rapport we'd struck with these strangers—the problem was that the leaving wasn't going according to plan, and if the plan was already fucked, then the rest of the trip surely would be because, for a trip to go well, it has to begin well.

A man called Dr. Dan was supposed to pick us up at ten that morning, outside the local hardware store. We'd load our bikes, head toward Des Moines, and be on our way to the northwest corner of the state, ready to start riding back across after a good night's sleep. The day before leaving, the two friends and I wondered what kind of bus it would be—one guessed a yellow school bus, another a Greyhound-style coach. Both possibilities were nauseating, the names alone evoking the sticky vinyl funk (yellow) and chemically cleaned bathroom sweetness (Greyhound) that would make reading impossible. The word, for either choice, was lurching.

Then Dr. Dan was supposed to pick us up at noon, then two, then four, then finally seven, when he showed up. I'd spent the day eating the snacks I was supposed to be eating on the bus, taking food-induced naps, and waking to an alarm that made me jump awake every time into a bedroom bright with sunlight from the west windows. Outside the hardware store, men tied our bikes to the ceiling of an enclosed trailer, which would be pulled behind the bus, and we drove off into the already-setting sun. Rick, our first back seat companion, introduced himself. I should clarify: These weren't seats; these were mattresses perched on some sort of ledge that was about a third the width of each mattress, so the front was always folding and pulling the whole thing toward the center of the bus. Rick apologized. But it's fun back here! he said, and explained that the bus had two kegs and we could pay for cups if we wanted and he'd been drinking since he got on, just west of Chicago, and boy, that bathroom was already a mess. Rick wore a Hawaiian shirt and black wraparound sunglasses, had a handshake that took too long to get rid of, legs shaved according to that odd bike-riding convention. Rick had done this all before, he said. Ask me anything, he said.

At least I'd left my apartment in good condition. I made sure to clean everything before I left, as I always do, and put everything away where it belongs—the plates in their metal cabinets, the clothes in their fiberboard drawers—thereby guaranteeing that there would be something tangible and exactly in order to return to. A bit of continuity, a ritual, a joyful habit.

We picked up a gaggle of bros in a suburb of Des Moines. They came with a thirty-rack of Coors Light and the aforementioned flamingo. They were loud and smelly and burped a lot, and I felt as if we were on a reality show, where all bros are the same and where the majority of the action takes place on a bus.

In the cabinets above us we found pillows to jam under the edge of our mattress to keep it from flopping forward and potentially launching us into the men's laps. During the half hour or hour when we'd effectively convinced our fellow passengers that we were asleep (and one of us actually convinced himself and legitimately was asleep), three of them began making fun of the fourth, who was from Brooklyn and therefore deemed "uptight." We learned he rode his bike in Prospect Park, worked some sort of tech job, and had Italian parents—a fact that came up after the bros began discussing that perennial white-people favorite: What are you?

No dude, you look like an Arab, like some sort of Iranian or something.

One of the others chortled; his friend explained: Dude, there's, like, a legit Iranian sitting right there.

He pointed with his eyes at one of my friends who, indeed, is Iranian.

Like a real Iranian, man. So shut up.

It had gotten cold since the sun went down, but if we closed the bus windows, the diesel fumes that were seemingly piped into the bus stayed trapped. Our busmates were drunk enough to pee with the door open; I was tired enough to fall asleep, briefly. It was so late; we were so late; we were going to get so few hours of sleep— about three at this point, by my estimation—which meant that the first day was already ruined.

I'm told it's virtuous to be spontaneous, that the characteristic is as much a mark of being a good person as is sending thank-you notes and bringing food to sick or sad friends. I'm still learning how to be flexible. And I don't think it counts as being flexible when I show up on time even though I know the friend I'm meeting is always ten minutes late, and when I show up each time and wait on the corner halfway between our houses unsure whether to wait on the sidewalk or the grass, I decide that next time I too will be ten minutes late but then, when the next time comes around, I chicken out for fear that this will be the one time she's not late but I am, and fear too that my tardiness will reinforce her habit and I'll be stuck again, waiting, except for twenty minutes.

This friend tells me I need to plan more spontaneity into my days, her suggestion mirroring the impossible dualism of modern digital-analog life in which unmeasured, unplanned unknowns are fun and also in which we're constantly given new ways to keep track as we're rushing through that exciting uncertainty.

On the bus, I texted friends about the shitshow of travels in order to hear back from them, and when I heard back, I analyzed the inflectionless tone of the replies, watching my departure from a screen remove. I wanted the present to be as controlled and settled as the past yet as open to my participation as the future. I wanted the leaving to end. Or I at least wanted to leave, briefly, as did a friend I studied abroad with in Spain. She once woke up on an airplane surprised to be on an airplane, no idea where she was going. So she asked a flight attendant: Canada. Yet again she'd taken a bunch of Ambien and stayed awake, pacing the Barcelona streets. Then she left. She was ok with it, she said after returning; it was fun.

Watching the dudes spit beer out of the bus window, the spray dotting the glass, the glass dotting the black night, I dreamed of leaving this way—not necessarily in a bizarrely adventurous stage of blackout but leaving just by leaving, without packing lists or waiting, just departure.

The flamingo man was asleep, the driver was falling asleep, and according to my phone, we were still hours away. Outside was dark and quiet except for the coughing engine and intermittent shudder as the driver drifted across shoulder rumble strips, each time correcting direction slowly, almost as if the movement in the opposite direction weren't a correction at all, just luck.

An interruption to my self-pity spiral: We were slowing down, pulling over, this time on purpose, stopping in the middle of nowhere, midnight, nothing in sight. A Coors Light can rolled past my feet, its Rocky Mountains thermochromic blue long gone. We were picking up someone called Falcon; he was always like this, they said—they being the voices from the front of the bus, up past the bathroom, past the empty kegs, around a bend (somehow the bus had a bend in it), these supposed voices of reason, supposed only because they were closer to the driver, who, we'd learn later, was a sweaty guy who couldn't read a map.

But, then, with the crinkling flutter of handwritten directions that filled in where dead phones couldn't, paper seemed to take over the front half of the bus. Some twisted their maps around, putting north on the right. Some left the orientation alone. Each person thrust his or her own sheet of paper over the others, layers flapping like paper airplanes coming to a halt at a wall. I always envied those boys in high school whose backpacks were messes of loose paper. No matter what, they could retrieve the single sheet they were after in one fell swoop of rummaging. Their calculators never had covers, their pens never had caps, but the screens were not scratched, and the ink never leaked. How did they manage such graceful disorganization? When they left their houses in the morning, did they double-check that their homework was part of the mess? I can't remember if I even did, but how could I not have? Just going to school every morning was a kind of leaving and therefore had to be properly set up by predeparture ritual.

The rituals vary, but they share a goal: Leave on a good note. For a trip, this starts with the packing list, with its unlabeled categories, items grouped on the page: clothes, cosmetics, fun things, less fun things, work things, last-minute things. Phone, computer, charger, wallet, keys, headphones, other headphones. Two pants, three T-shirts, two cardigans, underwear. The list is like stream-of-consciousness diary-keeping in reverse: If measuring the present is a way to control the future, then measuring the future, maybe, is a way to control the present. It's exactly inexact. But the way it redirects the focus from the trip itself, during which I might undergo change and things at home might undergo change or one or the other or neither, to the packing for the trip, which necessarily happens here, with things I know, in an order I know, with a list in my handwriting and on the same stationary (my dad's, from work) I've used forever.

I must have learned this somewhere.

The last step, always, is throwing away the list. To keep it would be sentimental. But you'd think I'd at least keep a master list—it would be dumb not to. I can't though, because the master list is not part of the ritual, and if I didn't have a list to make and then destroy, I'd be stuck with nothing to worry about besides time, and then I'd never leave at all, so bound up in considerations of time and space splitting for the trip and reuniting upon my return that that split would create a gap too great—too uncertain—to let open up in my absence. So I make the list, and on it I also write things to do before leaving: close windows, hide things, make bed, take out trash—implicit in that last item what "trash" includes.

And when I leave, I remember taking those last steps. When it comes to retrospective assessment, we remember, and we evaluate; we do neither especially accurately, tending to base assessments on the most intense moment of the experience and the end. In an experiment on pain evaluation, scientists had test subjects put their hands in a vat of cold water for sixty seconds. Then the subjects put their other hands in a vat of cold water for sixty seconds, followed by thirty seconds in ever so slightly less-cold water. When asked which experience they'd prefer to repeat, most said the second version, because though it lasted longer, and though it too contained sixty seconds of cold, it ended less unpleasantly. So when I'm leaving and feeling everything going to hell in a disordered handbasket but I have a tidy ending, so tidy that the list that kept it that way has been disposed of, I remember it differently. It becomes, when it's time to do it again, tolerable.

Falcon wasn't where he said he'd be, or he was and we weren't there. We'd find him at a bar after mile marker something, the neon Budweiser sign, pale in the bus headlights, marking a strange rural oasis—it was hard to hear over the bros' whispering, which was really more like talking (their talking more like yelling). I was still calculating in my head how fucked we were in terms of sleep, still thinking that knowing exactly how much sleep I'd lack would somehow make it better, but also knowing, simultaneously, that this trip was off to a bad start, plain and simple. The bus chugged, dripped in between the rumbles of the engine turning over again and again, dripped like Dr. Dan's back, dripped like the sweat that somehow was still on that warm Coors Light can, like the inside of the flamingo, like the sound of measuring, again and again, how late we were running: twelve hours and counting.

WAITING

could tell the woman running weigh-ins was sizing me up. As I stood on the scale, trying to look intimidating in spandex shorts and a sports bra, she looked at the number, looked at me, her eyes narrowing, looked at the number again, wrote it down. I thanked her, put my warmups back on, and walked to the locker room mirror, where I tied my bangs back so tightly I could hardly furrow my brow.

Outside, sitting at a table next to a rock-climbing wall, I pulled out my phone. The adrenaline of being at my first judo tournament in nearly a decade, plus the Coke Zero I'd finished by seven thirty in the morning, had my fingers fluttering so vividly that I could barely scroll. This, I decided, was the perfect time for the gas-station pizza I'd promised myself.

In a sense, I'd been waiting for this tournament for nine years, a period during which I first thought I would compete again, accepted that I wouldn't, and then didn't accept it. Tournaments were, and still are, mostly waiting, finding different ways to be uncomfortable in too-cold gyms and poorly lit hotel ballrooms and high-ceilinged convention centers, stepping outside into dense Miami air or prickly California breeze, warming up with teammates inside, the whole act choreographed, I hoped, for maximum preparatory power. There were always breaks, too, for stomach trouble.

At some tournaments, competitors were given match numbers, so the waiting at least was quantified and shortened. Studies have been conducted to prove the obvious: People are more comfortable when they're told how long they'll have to wait. With a number, I'd know roughly how long I could put off getting truly nervous, when I'd tell myself, in the moments right before matches, to win, that winning would take only five minutes of my life at most, like a slightly long song but silent, steeped in the almost mystical space of the spectated mat, where all sound except my coach's voice would slip away, slip off the world, the named world, the invisible everything where waiting held its breath, anthropomorphized into just another audience member I wasn't aware of.

I liked that mystical moment, but it took so much waiting to get there. I liked winning, but it required sometimes losing. I liked fighting, but so much nonfighting had to be endured—the travel times and sitting times and fretting times all heaped together into one barely bearable mass of uncertainty. It was worth it, but still, so much time waiting took its toll and turned the idea of competing into the idea of waiting, a false conflation technically, but theoretically right on the mark.

I didn't want anyone to see me eating the pizza because my hands were shaky and the bag the pizza came in exaggerated the tremor. When faced with interminable waiting, I eat with abandon. I eat as if it's something to get out of the way, the temptation and desire distracting enough to warrant quick and efficient removal. I give in every time, even though that distraction could mask the real wait, even though waiting to eat is the best kind of waiting: the kind that's entirely under my control.

I ate the slice in my sweltering car, windows up to keep the sweltering outside, car off because it didn't seem right to keep it running, and anyway, a running car, with its sweaty July chug, might call attention to the person in the car—the person eating pizza out of a fluttering bag, crinkling with nerves.

Back inside the tournament, I stood against a cinderblock wall and watched little kids roll around the main mat. I tried to calibrate the loops of uncertainty by telling myself I would win, don't think about it, but think about it a little bit, because, as a sports psychologist told me in high school, a little nervousness is a good thing. I addressed myself in the second person, pursed my lips and realized I was doing it only after the look on my face elicited from multiple half-strangers the question, Are you ok?

I had the same bag and warmup jacket as nine years ago, new gis, new black belt, new mouthguard, and, I'd find, if not a new take on waiting at least a slightly less jazzed way of dealing with it. I mean I did not get sick to my stomach. But I still had the same problem as before: All I could think about was not thinking too much about the wait—while also thinking enough about it to keep me on my toes. Performing requires at least a little anxiety to put me at the ready, but there is always the risk of letting the worry overflow into the kind of self-awareness—of full-bodied thinking—that guarantees a bad act.

I paced, I wandered outside, I came back in, and with the shouts of referees in the background, the occasional clap of a body hitting a mat, I sat on the Astroturf floor, against the bleachers, and closed my eyes and breathed, feeling time pass in sets of five minutes because timed judo matches have made me understand in my muscles what five minutes is.

I didn't take out my phone. This was my first tournament with a smartphone, and I expected the glowing gorgeous screen to be the perfect waiting companion. But everything could be a wrong move: Every text sent about the tournament could be a jinx, every thumb tap and swipe of dots-game dots could slice irrevocably through need-to-win concentration. (When asked, I say I'm not superstitious.)

The internet was too much. The network's potential trap might have webbed me in and away, the distraction that actually distracted or that added to the primary wait others, a hideous collection of waiting. So I hid the phone, continued telling myself, You will win (as I actually did), and not trailing off into the digital concerns of text messages and the world beyond the tournament, with its wires and beams and waves, its threats of unknowns no stronger than the tournament unknown but more plentiful and, therefore, more certainly too much.

The first match couldn't have arrived more perfectly. The first match of the tournament is the worst because the whole wait is, in a way, for it. And so it's also the best, because once it's over, the wait shifts, or at least diminishes. I fought, that day, in two divisions. The first, my regular weight division, arrived without warning: The tournament director walked over to where I shivered and asked if I was ready; they wanted to get some of the women's divisions out of the way. I had just a few minutes to warm up on a tiny square of mat, change into the blue gi, dance around on the side of the mat, keep the sweat going, focus, frown lips around mouthguard. It was ideal.

I asked the long-haired teen, the only other member of my judo club who was also there, if he'd take a few falls for me. He was a white belt; he had to say yes. We scurried over to the warmup mat, wedged ourselves in between other pairs doing the same thing, and fell into the rhythm of throwing they'd established, a sharp human metronome drowned out by the murmur of so many parents and coaches and players.

It's easy to get stuck in a loop while waiting to try to pummel a person. In between matches, I watched the other women warm up, and they watched me watching them watch me watch—and so on. The judo wait can be productive if you're good at intimidation: the practiced snarl of a serious face that exudes a confidence so exquisite and pure there couldn't possibly be any nervousness behind it. The gazes turn almost haptic when they meet, a direct link between the hectic hell of waiting (for me) and, when I'm not doing well at the waiting, her assumed calm (whoever she is).

I fought every woman there, I won, I left. I left on the three-hour drive with the teen boy, who'd missed his ride home. He couldn't believe I'd never been to Arby's. The twenty years I've been doing judo were unfathomable to him—probably because he'd been alive for only nineteen. We talked about God and souls and multiple universes, about parties and college (he's not especially interested in either). I gave him DJing duties and, when the same Supertramp song played for the third time, I wished I hadn't. It would have been so easy to just unplug his phone and switch to the radio while he was asleep, but I'd have felt bad, especially since he'd lost.

My traveling companion didn't mind lengthening the trip with an out-of-the-way detour to pick up my computer, newly repaired, from FedEx. Perhaps it's because, as he told me, he had no plans for the night—no one needed him home. In transit, time does not get wasted, only spent. There are certain rules of waiting that just are, maybe to make the rest of it manageable. Traveling, timelines sigh, relieved.

I was picking up the computer because I would have missed the delivery while away at the tournament and couldn't stand waiting till Monday, when there would be the possibility that the single hour I planned to be out of the apartment, at the gym, would be when FedEx showed up.

At the strip mall with the FedEx, when we stepped out of the car into the humid evening, I wondered what people made of the two of us, sweatsuited and with scrapes on our faces, a woman with a backpack, a boy tapping on his phone. The computer, it would turn out, was not actually repaired, and my winning streak would not last.

But as I put the computer box gently in the trunk and climbed into the sweat-stinky car, what would come next, that new unknown, didn't matter. I'd waited and I'd won. It didn't matter that I had work the next day, that I was relying on this teen to direct me down Iowa's gravel backroads to his house.

His was the driveway with the green pickup, he said. The house stretched its broad single story from a lone pine tree to a patch of grass. Farmland etched the background. Later, he said, stepping out of the car. Later, I replied.

DJ gone, I listened to the rocks flicked up into my car, the coda to the day.

Finally home, I draped my gis on the drying rack, doused them in whatever amount of Febreze justifies putting off doing the laundry for twelve to twenty hours, made myself pretty with powder over the mat burn on my forehead and a silk dress, and went out to celebrate the day with a friend.

The bar's jukebox thrummed alt-country music, lazy drawling guitars that suit a place where there's never a line at the pharmacy but there's a wait anyway, where business is slow enough at FedEx for the dude to recognize the computer box sent out a week before, where there's enough time waiting for everything that at the end of a years-long wait springs a crisis: What am I waiting for now? And how long will I have to wait to find out? And what will I do to busy myself while I wait for an answer?

And what if I decide the wait's not worth it? Then what?

BROADCAST

I went to bed while the party was in full swing, not listening to CCR and Rihanna and Bon Jovi and all the other music you'd expect at a house party at which the dominant snack was Nacho Cheese Doritos. I still hadn't told my boyfriend why, exactly, I was going to bed so early. I had yet to find a good opening.

We were in Nebraska for my boyfriend's college roommate's birthday party. I'd been traveling a lot lately, gone every weekend for a month, driving west and then north across a flat Midwest on the verge of fall, leaves trembling, the harvest in full swing, highways of trailers and shoulder-driving tractors. The land was yellow.

Before closing myself in the bedroom, I watched beer pong, I used a propane grill, I stared at someone unwrapping a package of drugs ordered on the dark web. Crowded into the attic bedroom, women in crop tops and men in basketball shorts rubbed powder on their gums and painted a giant sheet of plywood with green and red mushrooms speckled with beer foam. The rumble of voices from the floor below was just inaudible enough to be impossible to ignore. I felt at once very old and very aware of my limbs and how it was no longer comfortable to sit cross-legged; I could almost hear the reverberations of my tingling feet as they fell asleep below my knees. A cat crept by, and it was then, as it rubbed again my cuffed jeans, leaving thick orange hairs in their folds, that I decided I should call it a night. So I eased through the hatch and onto the narrow stairs and went in search of the master bedroom, where I'd left my things.

I slept in a sleeping bag on the bed in a room unchanged since the birthday boy's mom moved east and gave him this house, the house he grew up in. I slept, therefore, on a pink bedspread, on four pillows so flattened by time that they felt like one.

At two or three in the morning, a body popped through the door, then a voice: Are you really asleep? Who are you? Why the fuck are you asleep? I said nothing, waited. I really had been asleep, I was Rachel, and I was asleep because I couldn't be awake.

Or, more accurately, I really had been asleep, I was Rachel, and I was asleep because I couldn't be awake despite having pried myself there chemically and with will, despite knowing it was silly to drive five hours to a birthday party for someone I didn't know and then sleep through half of it, despite feeling bad the whole time, like I was letting my boyfriend down, and then feeling guilty for the guilt because it came from the ego-backed assumption that I was important, so important that fun depended on me.

But I shirked nevertheless. Sometime between getting in the sleeping bag and getting woken by the voice, my boyfriend had joined me, in his own sleeping bag, also on top of the bedspread, our awkward tableau reflected in the mirror in front of us against which were propped unframed family photos and stuffed-animal pigs. This would not be a good opening. Nor would the car ride back, nor the next day, during a break in bar trivia, nor the night before I left for the sleep conference, when it was just "the sleep conference," not the Narcolepsy Network Conference. Still, six years after getting a name for my tiredness, I couldn't say it in public. I couldn't say it because, in those years of not saying it, when most people thought sleep was just an excuse, or selfish and self-involved, I had come to believe them, and now it did feel like an excuse—and, at that, an excuse that could be truthfully described as all in my head.

At the conference, the preeminent narcolepsy researcher told us we're lucky we don't work like dogs: Narcoleptic dogs pass on the disorder in their genes, and those genes cause the disorder by ridding the brain of the receptors for hypocretin, a neurotransmitter that regulates wakefulness. Narcoleptic people, on the other hand, have the receptors but lack the hypocretin; their immune systems have destroyed the cells that produce it. Think of hypocretin as the key, the researcher said, and the receptors as the lock. It's much easier to replace a key than it is to make a whole new lock.

The disorder that's all in the head manifests itself in the body, especially for people with cataplexy, who get stuck in the paralysis of the dreaming body when they're awake. This is the stereotypical falling asleep of narcolepsy, which isn't actually falling asleep at all but a disconnect: The brain is awake, the person is conscious, but her body is paralyzed, as if being prevented from acting out dreams.

On a screen washed out by lights from outside the ballroom, the researcher played videos of kids keeling over, people barely able to walk they were so overtaken by cataplexy. Against the tan backdrops of hospital hallways and doctors' offices they dragged their legs over padded floors, tried to grip handrails tightly but could manage only to grasp at the metal as they might touch a cat. Their jaws hung low, mouths agape in the constant shock of being asleep while being awake. The audience hummed in recognition, looked at each other across wide-radiused tables covered by white tablecloths, nodded.

After the talk, people milled around the giant ballroom, weaving around tables and chairs, finding their seats with strangers or people they'd met last year, and finishing breakfast before the day's discussions began. Alice, a woman with dark, severely cut hair, sat down next to me. I wanted to meet Alice because I wanted to meet her little brown dog. She was talking to this dog as she placed her breakfast plate next to mine and said, looking down into fur-lidded eyes, Oh, you'll get your breakfast in a minute, honey—then, turning to me, smiling—*I* don't eat sausage.

How's it going? I asked. She was tired, she said, slicing the sausage into bite-sized pieces that the dog would later swallow whole; she wondered if her medication regime was losing its efficacy, wondered whether she'd make it till ten that morning without a nap; she'd slept twelve hours last night, she said, even skipped socializing with fellow conference-goers in order to be well rested the next day, the last day of the conference, but here she was, barely awake, so what was the point of all that planning? As she was telling me this, she took a bottle of Pepsi from her purse, set a clear, ice-filled Starbucks cup on the table, poured the frothy soda in it, and put the lid on, green straw poking out. Caffeine isn't enough, she said. Luckily it was cold in the hotel, and that discomfort had been helping to keep her awake, as discomfort has for me at bars, during movies, in school: I've refused cardigans in strong air-conditioning, painted peppermint chapstick under my eyes, and, back in high school, before I suspected anything was awry, when after-school naps seemed a luxury of second-semester senior year, nothing more, I'd pinch the skin on my hands until the backs of them were lined with fingernail half-moons haloed in blotchy red. None of it ever worked, so instead of perfecting a technique to be awake I worked out an in-school sleeping strategy: Pen in hand on paper, other hand supporting forehead, look down long enough while awake to establish that's just how I was sitting, and then fall asleep.

The woman and her dog and I walked side by side to the discussion on dreaming and creativity. The carpet absorbed our steps almost too well—Do you ever feel like your quads just don't work? Alice asked me. Yeah, like after taking a Benadryl, right? She nodded: That's how I feel right now. I don't know what's going on.

We peered into the room, and a woman beckoned us with her hands. Should I sit right next to the dog woman or leave a buffer? I wondered. People around us were hugging and laughing. I pretended to search my phone for something, and when I looked up the dog and its owner were passing through the doorway, the jingling collar faint against the soft pattering, like laptops closing, of tired people rushing in and out of rooms whose folding tables' seams grew wider and wider apart as the day went on.

Everywhere in the hotel, air-conditioning thrummed nonstop, the same tone as the outside air, which held the windblown hum of the interstate over which I walked three mornings in a row to get to the conference, crossing on a bridge bearing John Ashbery's poetry: "The place, of movement and an order." Construction flanked the highway, and in between the bulldozers and cranes waving against the flat gray sky stood a church whose electric billboard read "We are all under construction" in orange caps.

I kept expecting signs that something was off—people slackening in cataplectic collapse while talking, people walking extra slowly, people drinking coffee nonstop. And while there were slow walkers and coffee drinkers, there are everywhere. As for the lack of cataplexy episodes, said one of the researchers, who'd seen none this year, medication is so much better these days,

The only sign was our nametags. The first day, I walked to the registration table, didn't sign the photo release form, and then gave my name. Do you have narcolepsy? the woman behind the table asked. I leaned over the table, closer. Sorry? I said, because it was loud in the hotel hallway, or because no one has ever asked me that. People have asked if I'm tired, how I slept last night; they've asked if I have glasses, if I floss, if I have insurance. But not once has anyone asked if I have narcolepsy. The woman had asked because people with narcolepsy got ribbons that read "ZZZZZ" to attach to their name tags, dangling above and below other labels: Volunteer, Presenter, and, in my case, First Timer. (Non-narcoleptics weren't left out; they were labeled Supporter.) Each category came with its supposed characteristics—the caring volunteer, the benevolent-in-knowledge presenter—as if they were dimensions, each on its own meaningless, but together, like a height given a width and depth, made part of a full object: a person trying not to fall asleep.

I hesitated when I answered, caught off-guard, maybe, or maybe just embarrassed. To most people, I say nothing, afraid that my sleepiness, like theirs, will be renamed laziness. I pretend that I'm just a cautious person, one who goes to bed early and happens to work best in the morning. I'm a decent friend before eight at night, but after, I'm way too rigid to be much fun. This is who I am, except that weekend, at the conference, I wasn't; I was a First Timer, and I wore a ZZZZZ ribbon, those five gold Zs on an orange background proclaiming me the member of a very particular, nap-oriented in-group.

Every time I left the conference, I took the name tag off in the elevator, afraid that my label would somehow be legible to people who would, in reality, see it only as a bunch of Zs. To those people, I failed to tell myself, the Zs were not a measure of my pathological sleepiness; they weren't even a unit of measurement in the first place: They stabilized nothing.

At the dreaming talk I learned that you can be dreaming while awake—not daydreaming, not American dreaming, but in a nighttime dreamlike state in which you feel "you know everyone," "empathy is everywhere," and "creativity is the norm."

At another talk I learned that you can lie at work and say you have meetings when really you're asleep; you can request a standing desk, because falling asleep is easier while sitting. I learned you can still enjoy Blackhawks games with friends but if you leave early they'll think it's because you're bored or because they're bad company.

I learned that some conference rooms are colder than others, that more people in a room really do warm it up. I learned that scrambled eggs not labeled gluten-free might still have gluten in them. I learned that gluten is bad for you, that it puts you to sleep, that it doesn't put you to sleep, that it's good. I learned how to sit at a table listening to a conversation and seem both interested and like I wasn't listening in. I learned that it is indeed possible to get a caffeine buzz from a Frappuccino. I learned you need to schedule "me time," you need to put your needs first, you need other people.

I learned that narcoleptic tiredness looks and sounds an awful lot like regular tiredness, even when you're looking for a profound difference: People drink coffee and Coke and Diet Coke, people yawn, people nod off during boring presentations and movies, their heads dropping forward and popping back up like yo-yos.

I learned that the time of most empathy is the moment right before you fall asleep, when you're almost there, when talking would take you out of it but when not talking isn't even a conscious decision. Then, lying next to your partner, bursts of blue on eyelids with each nonblink—then, said the dream-talk psychoanalyst, is when "I love you" would mean the most, if only you could say it.

I learned I'd already waited too long to tell my boyfriend. According to conference consensus, I should have let him know on the third or fourth date; I should have found a moment, in between bites of pizza and sips of beer at the sticky-boothed bar with Cubs specials and a canoe on the wall. I should have found the moment and looked into eyes he calls gray but that are really blue, and I should have said, I need to tell you something. And then I should have told him. Or I should have told him on the car ride back from Nebraska, in between podcasts, or the day after, when we were in the cooler section of the grocery store. But even here, after saying the word over and over, when I tell myself to say it again, I can't.

DISEMBODIED

A t judo practice the other day, a man one hundred pounds heavier than me asked to go a round. I said, Sure, and told him, when he asked, how much I weigh (115 pounds), chuckled as he expected me to when he called me Fat Ass.

How, I wondered, could I be so open about my weight yet so secretive about how often I checked it? It's normal at practice for judoka to comment on each other's appearance, grabbing at arm muscles and stomach flab. After one practice, the intense consultant asked the laid-back physical therapist to press down on his spine to crack it. This? the physical therapist said, hands on the consultant's lats, This is too big. Too big? the consultant said, as if expecting a joke to open up. Yes, too big.

Bodies on display: over- and underdeveloped, starved, dried shriveled and hollowed for weight divisions. And then pumped back into color, bloated by the sudden return of food and water.

My first practice back home during college winter break, a friend from Turkey, a newcomer to English and thus forced into blunt and formal constructions, gave me a hug and then studied my face, considering its fullness. What happened? she said. Before-college Rachel (she sucked in her cheeks) and in-college Rachel (she puffed them out). One of the coaches brought up alcohol, and I didn't want to get into my high-school drinking habits, so I just agreed that yes, it was all the beer.

2.

I weigh myself on the days I'll like the number. The morning after an afternoon snack of brownies and ice cream at the office, empanadas for dinner, and little of my usual exercise, I didn't step on the scale. That Thursday, I was particularly concerned because I had a judo tournament coming up, and any fluctuation seemed loaded with significance—it could affect making weight, even the competition itself. And even more fraught was app-dating, which was steering me to bars and restaurants, where I don't have the willpower to exercise self-restraint.

When I do weigh myself, I want so badly to predict the future: As the scale flashes its horizontal bars, taking its time measuring, I guess what the number will be. If I can feel my stomach creased over the elastic waistband of the boxers I sleep in, I'll add a pound or two to my guess so I'm not surprised. The bathroom is always cold and my feet are always cold, and the plastic scale creaks under my weight. Maybe the L is hustling by in the background; maybe I can hear the automated voice caution against the closing doors. I keep my pajamas on because on the scale I've always kept my pajamas on. The zeros turn to dashes and the dashes to numbers and I'm either upset or I'm not. When I weigh too much I tell myself no dessert today, no alcohol. My weight laces the day with irritation: I snap at myself when my shoes don't look right, recoil sharply when the hair of the woman next to me on the train brushes my bare shoulder, and only later do I realize how very strong and obvious these manifestations of discontent are. Later, much later, like when I was out with Daniel and Jeffrey, who decided to order yet another round of dumplings, I thought twice but ate more anyway. I let my willpower fade away, encouraged by three or four weak cocktails.

3.

Girls in high school liked talking about metabolism. It felt scientific and unimpeachable. When I ordered a second sandwich at the sub shop, or finished off the bag of Milano cookies after school, they told me, You have a fast metabolism, as if I'd worked for it, like it was something to be proud of. I was proud, and so I ate.

The summer before senior year in high school, I was a counselor-in-training at the Wisconsin camp where I'd been a camper for years. All at once my fellow seventeen-year-olds and I had the freedom we'd yearned for as campers—staying up late, not ceding electronics to counselors, sneaking in boys, and, most pervasively and intensely, eating whatever we wanted.

I'd come to camp straight from Japan, where for two weeks the US's junior national judo team trained with Japanese high school students. I barely remember what we ate, and I can't remember if I ever weighed myself. There, we took communal showers and my body was placed relative to others, then relative to itself, as I worked out harder than ever before.

As a CIT, freedom meant ice cream cakes, candy, peanut-butter bars from the dining hall, contraband vodka and PBR, cheeseburgers during trips to town. I didn't notice my slowly expanding waistline because I wore mainly athletic shorts. But I suspect the idea of gaining weight wasn't even on my mind—it was unimaginable, a non-option.

4.

Sitting at the kitchen table in Anna's co-op apartment building, with a line of ants marching dutifully from the windowsill down to the baseboard, where they pecked at vintage crumbs, the low moan of video-game gunfire blended with jam-band bass draped behind the conversation, I said no to a second calzone: I have to get my bikini body for Mexico, I explained.

Know what she says about bikini bodies? Mitch asked, queuing up Anna for a punch line. Put on a bikini, Anna said, smiling, and that's your bikini body.

But when I looked into my bedroom's full-length mirror the next day, the sun strong through the blinds, this bikini body of mine was a pound or two over my weight-division cutoff, and all I saw was a lack of control. That night, lucky to have a body relatively privileged in public, I told myself I might as well keep eating cookies in order to erase future temptation. I'd already screwed up, so why not screw up more—a phenomenon I call the Fuck It Effect. Decisions I've made poorly, a judgment both circular and unhelpful.

5.

This is not about body acceptance, I tell myself every morning, I have no problems with that. Weight and age and so much of what women are taught to care about are just numbers, but inevitably they combine and in their union become a representation of a woman, one step removed. When the numbers change, so does the woman.

I am trying to locate blame.

You can deny the representation, say it is a copy but an imperfect one, like a flatbed scan of a 3D object, like when I held my poodle's paw on the scanner and watched his curls appear on screen, familiar but incomplete, lacking texture. My weight, in the morning, lacks texture.

6.

My parents had a scale when I was little, a metal oval with an analog dial and a needle that bounced into place. My grandmother's scale was fancier, black like all her clothes, manufactured by Thinner, a brand whose logo's text slimmed as the letters marched rightward. My grandmother bought the scale to follow what the word suggested. And then, when illness achieved it too effectively, to work backward, reading right to left.

7.

I remember distinctly being twenty-six kilograms because twenty-six kilograms was my weight division at my first Junior Olympics. I had to lose two-tenths of a kilo to get there, which I did by running on a treadmill in a sweatshirt, my Discman accidentally programmed to play the same song over and over, for twenty minutes. The song was "Come as You Are" by Nirvana.

No one thought of placing me in a division in which I was the smallest by ten or fifteen pounds, but yet how odd and inappropriate it seems to put a nine- or ten-year-old on a treadmill to lose weight.

I am finding fault in retrospect.

That is, I'm finding fault in the act of looking back.

At every tournament were mean-faced athletes drenched and dripping their way into lower weight divisions. They ran in hotel parking lots and crowded into hotel saunas; they wore scowls and wetsuits and trash bags. They went to the bathroom often. I rarely joined in. I always meet deadlines, as I say in job-application cover letters, and I'm usually prepared—which meant, for tournaments, that I'd aimed for my target weight weeks ahead of the competition, the goal stretched across time until it finally stopped at the weigh-in.

There were always two scales at large tournaments—an official one and a practice one. The practice scale might be out in the open, outside the curtained-off weigh-in area. Men and women, boys and girls stood amid a crowd of each other nearly naked, each competitor so focused on her number, she'd barely notice the others.

And what if the weight the two scales measured didn't match? These devices vary, even when they're fancy, with stickers guaranteeing their performance. Accuracy was always a concern, and murmurs in the crowd of gaunt-faced weight-cutters sometimes rose with news of a discrepancy.

That I can't remember who won that first Junior Olympics tournament—that's how centered I was on the treadmill.

8.

With Daniel and Jeffrey, sharing yet another dish—a doughnut—in a hipster Chinese restaurant-bar, as I wrestled my fork through the sticky pastry, Jeffrey, whom I'd met only a few weeks before, asked, Are you on your period or did you mean to take a piece that big?

I didn't know what to say, and I told him so, and he said sorry, he was drunk.

To those like him, a woman who lets loose her appetite is both mysterious and disgusting. To be a woman, then, is to fight against yourself: Ignore the appetite but also give in to what might be expected and spend a few days each month inhaling chocolate.

When women step on our scales, we remind ourselves of our responsibility, stay loyal to metrics, to their willpower-inspiring power. We quantify.

We do this all despite the fact that it's not cool to care about your weight; ignorance or nonchalance is better. We're supposed to live in the present. We're supposed to resemble models but never let on that we're aiming for anything other than our own goals for the body. We're supposed to weigh a certain amount, but we're not supposed to be so neurotic as to know whether we do.

9.

I asked Anna, a professor who studies women and their bodies, about weight, about whether it's uncouth for anyone—and women in particular—to talk about weight. It's uncool to say you're trying to lose weight, she wrote back. It makes sense: It is both uncouth and uncool to talk about losing weight because it is uncouth and uncool to be fat, to have a body that, according to popular opinion, is a reflection of poor willpower, a body out of control. Women, Anna added, now call dieting "getting strong," a kinder term that's just as much about control as any other.

We've found acceptance imagining our diets as a traditionally masculine activity. Without the act, we're prone to the whims of bodies that bleed monthly, whose hormones rise and fall and whose stomachs bloat. The mind too is forever associated with these cycles—moody, irritable, ever on the brink of sad-eating a pint of ice cream. Mind and body inextricably tied, the mind is blamed for the body's shape and the body blamed for the muddled mind. She loses control because she's a woman. She can't help it.

10.

Sitting beside us at the Chinese restaurant was a group, one of whom, the one in the cable-knit sweater, announced he would attempt the restaurant's challenge, the Bao Bomb: Eat fifty pork buns and a bowl of soup in under forty-five minutes. "Challenge" made the competition ready to be memed. It was distinct from a "challenge food," something revealed to me at an "etiquette dinner" during my college's senior week, an event my friends and I had attended because we wanted free food. A challenge food, the dean of the college explained, as we all applied scare quotes in our heads, was messy, required fine cutlery skills; one should not eat a challenge food at a work meal. She added, Never finish all the food on your plate, be the first one to take something from a shared plate, or have seconds. Eating must be delicate. We ate wedge salads and pasta coated in tomato sauce that was likely ketchup.

She went on, Never announce when you're going to the bathroom. Just excuse yourself, because everyone knows where you're heading. Manners, it seemed, denied the very reason we eat: because we're hungry. And though it was a room of all genders, the rules seemed particularly directed at the women. Of course, real women don't shit.

I don't remember if the sweatered man conquered the Bao Bomb. What matters to me is whether "challenge" comes before "food" or after.

11.

Uneasy and stoned, I felt as if I were watching a TV show. Then I wouldn't have had to interact with the twenty or so people around me and risk overemoting—laughing too hard, wildly enthusiastic about a hare-brained idea, empathizing more strongly than I deserved to. Steph commented on my outward stoicism as we stood in the smoke-filled garage and acted like high schoolers when really we were a bunch of grad students ashamedly and shamelessly celebrating April 20. You always look so serious when you smoke, Steph said, and I forced myself to smile, as if that single grimace could prove her wrong. Next to us, men we recognized from the grad-student bar argued about the merits of austerity in Germany while one of them tried to light a cigarette with a glowing piece of waxed string. I was growing hungry again. I guess so, I said.

I reached across the table for the puffy Cheetos and, after wiping my hands on a paper towel, started rolling a joint. My fingers were cold; the cool spring night had fully eased in through the garage's uninsulated walls and wrapped itself around us, standing there at plastic folding tables topped with bowls of cookies, boxes of pizza, and lighters. I was long past the onset of the Fuck It Effect, exhaling smoke and inhaling orange snacks. Smoking made eating acceptable, or reasonable, the way menstruating did. Whereas the former allowed me to give in to appetite without giving up agency, the latter was just something that happened to me, that occurred in my uncontrollable and uncontrolled body.

I tried to stay steady. I stopped myself from giving in and talking endlessly about 3D-printed pants; I stopped myself from giggling until I wept. When I got home, I dutifully hung up my clothes and fell fuzzy-mouthed into bed. I considered all I had eaten, and I felt for a moment triumphant like a man. The next morning, when I woke sober, I was back to plain old regret. So I stepped onto the scale and waited for those numbers to preempt appetite.

SWEAT

When I really started sweating, it came from the tops of my hands and behind my knees. It came from my earlobes and back, and on my lips it dawdled before falling to the floor, where it gathered in a puddle that glistened on the steam room's tiles. Around me people breathed heavily, air moved visually, and a hangover seeped from my pores. The thick air menaced, held a heat wet enough to cause sweating to start more or less upon entering the room, or at least to seem like it did, as the body gained a coating of dew.

Hell is hot. The deserts that drive people to insanity are hot. New York subways in summer, too many layers in winter, rushing through airports, embarrassment—it's all sweat-inducingly hot. So is the steam room, a space people willingly walk into, where they sit down, hunch over or lean against hot walls, and breathe like they've been condemned or stuffed with phlegm. I began willingly walking in last winter, when, bored one Saturday, I thought I'd do what the man I had a crush on did and go spend some time in the steam room. He made the activity sound virtuous. Often when we'd hang out—the rare times he didn't cancel at the last minute, claiming that he'd had a breakthrough in his novel, promising he'd read it to me next time—he'd tell me how he'd just gotten back from an hour-long steam room session during which he'd solved the meaning of life or explained the singularity, or something. Meanwhile, I'd usually be coming off an hour trying to send enough emails to make me feel useful, to make time feel worthwhile, to have something to show for it.

The first time I went into the steam room, the two shirtless men already inside were breathing loudly, deliberately. I peered in on my way to the locker room, looking through the tinted windows to see if any women could offer me outfit cues. The two men sat across from one another, arms plopped down on thighs covered by baggy basketball shorts that dangled over flip-flops for one and sneakers for the other. I figured a sports bra, running shorts, and the deck shoes I'd worn to the gym were equivalent. Sliding a quarter into a locker, I felt conspicuous, like everyone could tell I was at the gym for the sole purpose of not working out.

The two men panted. I sat down, thought they were being a bit dramatic, but then the novelty wore off and the heat and dampness fell around me and on me, heavy and impossibly full. My shorts were soaked within minutes. I sat, back rounded, watching the wet air and my own sweat mix and drop down into the creases in my stomach, then into my shorts waistband. I was glad the shorts were black; it made the saturation harder to notice. But there in the room, steamed into submission, sweating wasn't something to be embarrassed of. It couldn't be: The room itself, with its faucets spitting vapor and drips dropping from the ceiling and drains lackadaisically taking in the slow-streaming rivulets tracing tiles downhill—the room itself was sweating, and to walk into a place so atmospherically demanding without giving in to that atmosphere seemed irresponsible, or at least disrespectful.

Oddly, in the gym, sweat is still something to be erased. To leave a trace of oneself in the shape of an ass or back print dripping down the black vinyl of a machine or bench is rude at best, unhygienic at worst. Gyms have towels for mopping one's face, for getting rid of sweat beads before they become too full and fall to the floor, where they either evaporate or get soaked up and pushed around by mops.

I've long been ashamed of how much I sweat, and I've long loved sweating. When I was little, at judo practice, I'd envy the adults whose faces were lined with moisture. They'd leave little trails of liquid on the mat, their pants darkened at the knees and waist. Then one day it happened: I looked into one of the mirrors along the side of the mat and saw a lone bead of sweat making its way down my cheek. I smiled; the sweat bead, up against my raised cheek, paused, then fell to the ground as I let my face ease back to neutral.

Sometimes the judo coaches would chide the class if we weren't sweating sufficiently—we must not be working hard, they'd say. Even now, even in winter, if I leave judo practice with a shirt damp only in the small of the back, I feel like I haven't done enough. But then other times, particularly outside of sports, it takes no work at all to become drenched. It took me much too long to understand the importance of color and fabric; it took until a soaking night in my early twenties to understand the hazards of light gray. A friend and I were walking from my fan-cooled apartment to an outdoor bar. It was July. New York was still with heat. About twenty minutes into the walk, I hit the point of no return: I was going to ruin my dress. On empty street corner I ducked to the side of the former office-supply store, now mostly vacant save for white metal shelves and reams of paper, and reached up the dress to dry my stomach and back with a handkerchief, the same one I used to dab my face in subway tunnels. My friend kept watch from the busier street, where traffic wove around dump trucks and cranes outside the new stadium. A plastic bag rustled by, bouncing across the sidewalk and over the curb. The sweat kept coming no matter how much I blotted, and I began to suspect that the act of blotting was actually taking enough energy to make me sweat more.

At the bar, outside on the patio's park benches, I sat up straighter than ever, arms held slightly out from my sides so my forearms could rest on the table like I was a king holding a scepter. A friend held his glass of icy whiskey and ginger ale against my neck. I sucked on rough-edged ice cubes. Then I excused myself and went into the single bathroom where I saw it, my savior: an Xlerator hand dryer. After checking that both of the door's locks were secure, I took off the dress and held it under the jet of hot air, trying to keep my body away from the heat. I didn't look in the soap-spattered mirror at my warped reflection, didn't look down at the black bra saturated with sweat; if I didn't see myself nearly naked in a bar bathroom, then maybe I wasn't nearly naked in a bar bathroom. After a few minutes, I myself was still clammy, but at least the dress was dry, its dark streaks and patches faded away.

I used a similar technique on other nights, when, before going out, I'd check my shirt's armpits and, if they were damp, I would blast them with a hair dryer. It's not ironic that the solution to wetness caused by heat is more heat; it's just unfortunate. If only we could accept sweating, I'd think in those moments, falling into a fantasy of blotchy T-shirts and shiny noses. But no, the body cannot show its unruly tendencies—it cannot let on that the mind within is not always the boss.

Sweat marks the nervous, the uncomfortable. It marks the

panicky and the late. It is a measure, always, of something—context dictates exactly what. But when that sweat is so obscured by place, overshadowed by the purposeful humidity and the sweat-stained intentions of a space like the steam room, it no longer functions as a measure of a person's internal state. It no longer functions as anything; it doesn't even serve its purpose, for that matter, of cooling the body through evaporation. In the steam room, nothing can have any purpose, and what production there is—of sweat, of breaths— has no measurable bearing on anything. In the steam room, one has no control, not even over temperature, only the option to leave.

That first day, I sat in the steam room, one man on either side of me, wasting time, aware that I was wasting time and maybe feeling guilty until it became too hot to be aware of much more than the question of how I'd gone this long without steam rooms. How could I have accepted the constant push into productivity without trying to find a place that prevented the production of almost anything, not least of all data? My breathing grew louder, sounded panicked, and I thought maybe I should be more nervous about getting stuck inside. But as soon as I began to create the scenario—we'd stay hydrated by licking the floor—I'd lost it to the heat.

The novel-writing man goes to the steam room because he thinks it helps his novel-writing. A friend from my judo club goes when he needs to lose weight, an unfortunate addition of the explicitly measurable to the space. Another friend goes not to contemplate plot or shed pounds but to fuck strangers. His face blurred by vapor, he communicates with his body, with movements both furtive and obvious, a language derived from the outside world but specific to this inside one.

And me—I go there to do nothing. Novels, weight loss, sex—none of it is the aim of my steam room time. The aim is to have no aim. For me the steam room, with its tiles and low light, its two-tier seating and arrhythmically dripping faucet, is the one place where I can sit and do nothing without feeling any urgency, without feeling any need to be productive, no need to even think. Bludgeoned by hot humidity, I go slack with exhaustion despite my stillness; I feel energized too. I stop noticing passersby through the fogged-glass door as the world outside the room fades into the clear air and I fall into something like the trance of musical improvisation or the liminal gap between waking and sleep that comes clear only after it's closed, only after.

I sit and I sit, unsure how long I've been inside or how much longer I'll stay, unsure how much I've sweated, how red my face is, unsure that I'm even doing my muscles any good at all. And that is the point, that uncertainty, that unquantifiable everything of the place, the place dense with no expectations, dense with voids. I think of nothing—no, I do not think.

When I'm ready to leave, I do, and the world comes blasting back as I hit the cold air just past the door. There, I lose my steam-addled sense of time, a sense that's stretched and wrinkled like a balled-up shirt—which is to say, a time that gives in to the environment, not the other way around. On the way home, everything can be counted again; everything can count: I think of the errands I must run, of the emails I must send, I wonder how much I could've gotten done that morning had I not gone to the steam room. But then I stop myself: The steam room was part of my routine, and as such, it was the responsible place to spend part of my morning.

When I told one friend that the steam room at the student gym I go to is coed, she pushed her chin back into her neck, breathed in, said, It is? I answered by saying, It's not weird, really—really. There's an etiquette, I explained, like in an elevator. In both rooms, people begin shifting positions as soon as the door cracks open, adjusting so no one space between people is larger than any other space. The production of gaps between people is choreographed without a choreographer. And that's it—that's all that happens. There, devoid of responsibility, the steam room holds leisure time, sweats it. If leisure is the purpose, though, then is finding that leisure, in a sense, productive? Or am I just looking to theoretical nonsense to make my time steaming worth something?

At first I expected that I, like the novel-writer, would emerge with a breakthrough, would have to run out of the room and to my locker, stopping to dry my hands before tapping into my phone whatever groundbreaking, paradigm-shifting thought I'd thought. I looked forward to it. Disappointment set in almost immediately, as I realized that not only would I lack groundbreaking thoughts—I'd lack thoughts at all.

But was that so bad? Was that not pretty good, pretty mind-blowingly wonderful? The thrill, maybe, was half from sweating, half from doing nothing but sweating. Finally, a place to do the two things I so often yearned to do: to sweat without shame, and to discount everything.

WIND

When lightning hits water, the electricity spreads outward across the surface. The mast of our boat was an especial problem much the way a lone tree is: With its tendrils of positive charge, it called to the polarized clouds, literally reaching for them.

The forecast was wrong, of course. The rain that might've come that afternoon (60 percent) came in the morning (0 percent), five hours ahead of schedule. My parents and I were a mile from shore when the air changed: The wind died, and from our boat until halfway to the horizon Lake Michigan turned glassy; beyond, waves like corduroy lined the water with consistent and constant rows. The stillness around us was soft in light too dark for ten in the morning. We panicked.

This was before weather apps, when people still used BlackBerrys, before hyperlocal forecasts with numbers that are still wrong, apps that say, No rain anywhere in the area, despite windshield wipers wiping and raised umbrellas puffing inside out— despite the precipitation exactly in the area. When this happens I'm not frustrated but hopeful: The weather just needs to catch up with the app, the reality with its measurements. Nevermind that a forecast is a measure of the future, not the present.

Still, I have a deep affection for weather forecasts. On my phone every morning, standing in front of my desk, towel wrapped around my wet hair, I check two apps, then three sites on the computer, computing by intuition some inexact average that helps answer, among other things, which shoes to wear and how many pairs of socks. I need weather—its numbers, its icons—for decision-making, and I need decision-making for movement, for not being stuck in a bathrobe, staring into a closet of unquantified possibility, or in front of the mirror, trading one cardigan for the other, unable to decide which one looks best and if it looks good enough to trump temperature concerns.

And there is knowing the weather for social reasons too, so I have something to say when I step into an elevator and lock eyes with someone I sort of know. We face the front, arms at our sides, and in winter we tell each other we're cold and in summer we say we're hot and in between we find something distinctive about the day—the humidity, the wind—to complain about.

If you sail too close to the wind, the sail flickers back and forth and the boat doesn't just stop but moves in reverse. Sail too far from the wind, and the sail again luffs, sometimes swinging the boom all the way around, the sound of the thwapping canvas like punching. But sail just close enough and the sail grows taut, the centerboard hums through the water, and the boat glides miraculously forward.

The wind that morning was from the west, from behind the city's long-toothed skyline, which meant to head straight away from the beach, downwind, we'd have to let the sail all the way out. We arrived at the beach right when the sailboat-rental place opened. Seagulls pocked the sand, pecking at trash. A shirtless guy with a faint life-jacket tan dragged the flat-bottomed 14-foot Sunfish knockoff down to the water, where he flipped it over and tied the mast upright while we cinched tight sun-bleached life jackets that smelled like seaweed, sweat, and an old basement. We'd have to wait to put the rudder and splintery centerboard down until we were in the water, deep enough that the wood meant to keep us going straight wouldn't get stuck in the sand.

I'd been sailing for a decade, mostly at summer camp in northern Wisconsin, where we'd play pirates on a lake whose other side— the peeling birches, the spit of sand and rocks—you could easily see from the shore, while learning the nuances of sail trim and the wind clock, a conceptual diagram that dictates how far out the sail should be when the boat is pointing a certain way relative to wind direction. Before heading out, rowing in a sea-green rowboat from the dock to the boat, I'd find direction in the hulls: Boats tied to buoys point into the wind. How stiff the flags on the camp flagpole were—how loudly and crisply they thwacked into perfect rectangles—and how dark the water was, told me speed. If there were whitecaps on our small, glacially cut lake, it was windy, and if the whitecaps were surrounded by black water, it was too windy.

Later, I saw wind in numbers, too unsure of instinct alone to make the decision whether or not to head out, albeit on a bike, not a boat. Surrounded by rural farmland, I wouldn't go if the weather sites told me the wind was blowing faster than ten mph, though in a city I would, because in a city there are buildings for the air to bounce off of and slow, there are packs of people breathing the wind in and out, the whole whir overtaken by cars and subways and the sounds of relative density, the music of movement. But in cornfields, especially when the corn was gone, when the fields looked like they'd been trampled by giants, then the wind blew faster than ten mph even when Wunderground.com listed it as such. Accuracy depended on harvest, on straightaways and hills, it depended on what I was used to, and it depended on all the people who could be there if the land weren't growing insufferable bounty insufferably fast, and if the pace there supported more than one post office per town.

When the wind blew from the south I rode north, up the road I lived on, past one neighborhood of half-empty subdivisions, another encircled by golf courses, neon green in summer and snow-bright in winter, then a slight westward slant before I turned around. Near the turnaround point, I passed a field bare in all seasons, open and vast for the wind to rush across. The water tower beckoned from ahead, a shadow cast on the low church beside it. My phone in my bike-jersey pocket, pressed flat against my back, traced my route on a map, and though it got the distance right, there was always an anomalous peak in the speed graph, putting me at forty or forty-five miles per hour when I knew I couldn't have been going faster than thirty. Sometimes one of those construction-area speedometers standing on the side of the road would clock me going my usual fourteen or fifteen miles per hour, and I would wonder if the cars that passed me noticed, if they thought my legs were spinning too fast or too slow for such a speed, whether the speed looked natural, or if they didn't notice at all, barely even seeing the bike as they sliced by and interrupted the wind so it built into a heavy thump that came five seconds later, after the cars disappeared around one of the many rolling-hill bends that kept me thinking about stray pebbles, dew-slippery leaves.

Every moment of sailing is a decision. Am I tacking efficiently upwind? Time the turns by glancing at the digital watch I wore only at camp, the one with the green band that never felt tight enough. Am I pointed exactly where I want to go? Draw imaginary lines tracing trajectory. Have I decided in the first place where that is?

My parents and I had nowhere in particular to head, so we just went out, zigzagging our way away from the shore, moving vaguely in the direction of the water-treatment plant. The lake was August green-blue, clear enough to see down twenty or thirty feet, way deeper than I ever want to touch; I'm afraid of underwater things. Their sliminess alarms me.

We'd picked that morning in particular because we had no other time to go, because the wind didn't seem too strong, because we wanted to, and in the face of an undaunting yet imperfect forecast, we thought our confidence would be enough to ward off storms. I'm decent at sailing; my parents trusted me. My parents are decent at the wind; I trusted them. They taught me the wind bike-riding: First ride against the wind and then, heading back, with it. A friend I ride with thinks it's a silly habit, that it doesn't matter when the hard part comes because it'll be hard at some point no matter what, and how much difference does the wind make, anyway? So much, I tell her, and she goes where I want to go first because she's a good friend and, to her, direction doesn't matter. She too checks the weather, but she's spontaneous, and when the forecast is wrong, and she's without the right jacket and cold, she doesn't kick herself. She doesn't even kick the weatherman. She just keeps going, cold, but sure she'll warm up sometime soon.

On the lake, air dead, one of us decided we should turn around and head back, trying to beat what was quickly becoming a thunderhead. My mom says I made the choice, but picturing myself with tiller in one hand, mainsheet in the other, parents facing me, their knees touching and feet crowded in the shallow boat, I imagine it was less a choice and more instinct, the physicality of sailing saving me from overwrought intellectualized decision-making. I am best at physical choices, in games or sports, when the key is not thinking; otherwise, when the key is thinking, but thinking just enough, I'm a mess.

The thunderhead filled the sky, a sky the color of a salted asphalt road in winter, the stillness like the morning after. The sail sighed. Its tension gone, its shape bent not by the wind but by the nothing left by stilled wind. Maybe the storm would disappear as quickly as it had come, I suggested as we barely moved. My mom's eyes were wide.

I pumped the rudder against the flat water, my hand a blur in the windless air. My life jacket rubbed against my upper arms. What do we do? I asked again and again. Just keep going, my dad, ever calm, said. He wondered if he should jump out to swim, but then what if lightning struck the water, forgoing the temptation of our metal-tipped boat and plunging straight down into the lake.

The first time I tipped in a sailboat wasn't at camp but there on Lake Michigan, in a sailing class, only a mile or so north of where my parents and I were fighting the oncoming storm. I remember seeing the sail and then being under it, I remember being cold. I remember being told, years later, that if you ever get trapped under the sail, you should follow its seams outward.

I remember us thrashing on the lake, arguing about what to do and about how far we were from the shore, yelling over the silence.

The wind knocked the boat sideways in a single blow. Air slapped the sail and then the sail was scooping water and the centerboard was flinging a wide arc and we were holding on to the hull, our legs underwater. Get under the mast! I yelled to my dad, hoping he'd prevent turtling. He held it afloat with his life-jacketed torso as I climbed onto the centerboard to flip everything right-side up. The boat wobbled back, and we climbed in, trying not to see the lightning nearing, trying not to hear thunder snapping the empty air, but we were the only ones on our section of the lake, and the swells of calm punctuated by swells of blowing pulled all our attention to how very unnatural those states are.

It was not fun, that fleeing from the storm. And it was my fault: I'd been the one who wanted to go sailing in the first place. No matter that my parents had agreed, that my dad had deemed the weather safe and my mom had deemed the weather safe, that we were all there together against a bout of unpredictability, not intention; no matter, because I was responsible for the day being fun and now I was responsible too for us not dying—and the melodrama of thinking that's what might happen.

How could we have trusted such inaccurate measurements? How could I have accepted a prediction based on who knows what, maybe some radar, or something I hadn't even checked?

Another slap, and again we were sideways, we were in the water, we were all saying, I don't know what to do what do I do? while moving somehow in unison, as if bound by panic. I leapt on the centerboard again and again, crawling toward it and heaving my torso onto its slimy side, righting us only to tip, the lightning cracking nearer and nearer to where we were now rocketing through the water toward the breakwater, where the suntanned sailboat guy was reaching out, his palms open, for the boom of our boat, where he was jumping in, and where another guy, raincoated and in flip-flops, grabbed us by the shoulders of our life jackets and leaned back, dragging us one by one up onto the pier. Run! he said, and we ran, and my cheeks, hot with embarrassment and failure, burned against the needling rain. By the time we were back on the beach, wet and shaky, the suntanned guy was climbing out of the boat near the beach and walking it up onto the sand, the wet painter rope dripping a dotted line that was soon erased by the bottom of the boat mashing the sand smooth.

We were walking, we were moving, the storm was gone— which was luck, whereas the situation itself was all my doing, a statement that even then I didn't quite believe, despite suspecting, in narcissistic backup, that nothing that can be measured, even inaccurately, happens by chance:

Lightning never strikes the same place twice. If you bring an umbrella it won't rain. Opening an umbrella inside will bring bad luck. A single woman who picks up an umbrella she's dropped will be single forever. If cows turn away from the wind, rain is on the way. If cows lie down, rain is on the way. If a cat cleans behind its ears, rain is on the way. Low-flying swallows mean bad weather; hiding spiders mean rain. Cutting your fingernails on a boat will bring storms. Whistling will bring storms. If a storm comes while a dead person is being buried, it doesn't bode well for the dead person's soul. Busy ants are a sign of bad weather. Busy dolphins around a boat in good weather are a sign of bad weather. Hogs weep when a storm is near. You can hear the drowned when a storm is near.

COMMUTE

MONDAY

My back fell asleep against the blue felt, and next to me a woman let off alternating wafts of coffee or cigarettes. My book, chock full of citations at the end, ended early, so I looked out the window at the Target, post office, trees, gravel under the tracks marking the entrance into the suburbs. A graveyard shifted past the east window, and two women talked about texting their boyfriends. I was sure I didn't leave the backdoor unlocked, but maybe the faucet was dripping, and maybe my bedroom light was on. Every two weeks at work we talk about guitar cases; this would be one of those days. I let my eyes close in between the last two stops, wondered briefly where I'd end up.

THURSDAY

I finished *The Executioner's Song* on the way home last night. Now I'm reading a hardcover, which tires my thumbs. I caught a later train than usual but still made my connection; I spent one or two minutes on my way to the first train retracing last night's steps from my car to the front door, looking for the bracelet I'd put in my pocket with my keys, a bracelet that I knew I'd lose when taking my keys out, but told myself that, because of the knowing, I wouldn't actually lose it.

MONDAY

This morning I tried a new train. I'm nearly done with my book, and I'm dressed for an air-conditioned office in long underwear in summer. This morning I waited for a message back; we're texting about music. On the train I had plenty of room and no sunlight to warm my thighs. A woman nearby murmured into her earbuds' cord while propping open a book about success. I hit my head on a dangling strap at my stop. I chose the righthand stairs, the turnstile second to the left. Crossing the street, I didn't mind making cars wait. Teens skateboarded around the war memorial, and a man clutched an e-cig in his fist.

TUESDAY

I came out of the book to Marshall sitting across from me, his sunglasses on and Birkenstocks frayed at the toes. For the first time in a week, I didn't fight sleep. I asked Marshall how band practice turned out as we squeezed through the crowd down the stairs and onto the sidewalk, into the air thick with last night's rain.

MONDAY

I dodged coworkers on the train platform and stairs, past the Dunkin' Donuts and into the street, where a car threatened. In the elevator we all took off our headphones and said hello. Marshall faced the back of the elevator, which I frowned upon, perhaps too literally.

WEDNESDAY

The book woke me as it flopped forward in my hands. I came from the dentist this morning, walked into the sun on the way there and, as these things go, away from the sun on the way back. I swiped through Bumble on the L platform and wrote a message as I sat on the train. I glanced at the screens next to me—Instagram—and wondered how self-conscious I should be with this dating-app interface displayed for my seatmates to see. Maybe they could help me with my opening line, which didn't seem to be that appealing, based on the return responses—or lack thereof.

FRIDAY

Maybe the Mitski album is the best album of the year. The opening pun is arresting.

MONDAY

We all arrived at the same time, me and my coworkers—the two I can't stand, the two who smirk and smile. Their voices bother me, their shoes bother me. That they bother me bothers me. Most days, they come to work with wet hair. Man or woman, it doesn't matter.

TUESDAY

I bristled particularly at the man on my left, whose arm was pressed firmly into mine; I imagined I could feel the creases of his suit jacket and his muscles beneath. On my left a woman had the last seat next to an open space and could have shifted leftward so our arms didn't touch, so her bag straps didn't drape on my thigh, but she did not shift, and the man on my right pressed on, and all through the train ride I thought mostly of the literal warmth of strangers.

WEDNESDAY

I was so tired that I considered skipping the gym, but on the train I didn't fall asleep once; the book was tense. On the way to the office the heel tap fell off my shoe so I pried off the other one, so fearful of the uneven walking I didn't even take a test step before removing the plastic half-moon. I'd have to get new taps; I'd do it over lunch. I'm a heel-heavy walker and can never remember how to spell "heel." I'd like to heal my worrying ways, mold them into preparation rather than anxiety. I set alerts on my phone because it makes me feel like I'm getting things done. I set one for taps. I could pretend I wasn't thinking about taps.

TUESDAY

The purple line peeled away from Wellington and crept toward Belmont, throwing its headlights into the morning sun. Sweat beaded on my nose and fell from my elbows. I felt it inch down my back as I stepped into a car that was, for once, not over-air-conditioned. Next to me a man readied his phone for a photo of Wrigley Field, and as he posted it to Instagram, I examined his shoes—did his girlfriend choose them? I remembered buying shoes for Chris' birthday and again for Christmas, and Nick too, and I thought about these boyfriends as possibilities, somehow still open, as if I hadn't ruined it and broken up with them.

TUESDAY

The train was early this morning and empty. No stranger's hair brushed my bare shoulder; my shoulder wasn't even bare. The sky split over the North Side into rain and light; the train's windshield wipers wiped preemptively, or predictively. Before transferring, I stood across from a woman and pretended to send emails on my phone instead of watching her caress a man's stomach, his monogrammed sleeve just below eye level. I wondered if the tattoo on her foot was designed to follow the line of her flip-flop or if the parallel was a coincidence.

THURSDAY

I was sleep-flung, so I propped myself against my book against the pole and hoped I wasn't drooling too much. I slept through most of the new Frank Ocean album, which has less to do with the album and more to do with breakfast, a late night, the foreboding heaviness in my gait, a familiar roughness to my steps. I fantasized, as I often do, about remaining on the train. Today's details could be any day's details—their general shape sanded smooth by repetition and the tedium inherent in sitting and watching.

WEDNESDAY

I dreamed last night about catching a bedbug in a Ziploc bag that wouldn't seal. I woke in a sweat, and then it was time to take a shower and consider cutting the security tag out of my new shirt, time to leave early, avoiding the regulars on the platform: the man with the big nose, big neck, the triceps horseshoed to perfection. Or the woman with the khaki pants and backpack. I woke to a mist glare speckling suburbia.

MONDAY

I can't stop looking at their rings. They have single diamonds and three diamonds, they are gold and silver on women and titanium on men. I try to guess how old the wearers are and how far behind I am. I have no one around to witness my bad habits; I want someone there when I'm plucking my eyebrows.

WEDNESDAY

Power cut "due to an unauthorized person on the tracks at Sheridan." Not upset about being late, I returned to my book about empathy. Perhaps we can't empathize with someone awful, the author writes, because we're trying to protect ourselves from what's familiar in him, what we might share, that awfulness. The train moved on. As we streamed by Sheridan I saw orange-vested CTA people with their hands on the shoulders of a man bent over, bowed towards the wooden platform. He tried to kill himself, I thought, making him unauthorized, though the word "unauthorized" felt unnecessarily formal. I didn't even consider empathizing; I knew only that I would be late, and I was glad for it.

TUESDAY

A man replaced his zipper pull with a large paper clip. Why I don't keep my train card in the outside pocket of my wallet I don't know.

FRIDAY

A consultant dropped the inside of his *Wall Street Journal*, then let go of the whole thing. He swung with the train, umbrella slipping from under his briefcase handle, where it was unsuccessfully wedged. A woman picked it up and handed it to him. He wore, like many midtwenties corporate men, brown shoes and blue pants; he looked attractive but in an unattainable way. By the end of the trip, I wanted to lock eyes with him.

WEDNESDAY

The train was phlegmy, a rattling cough, wet. Passengers wore the coats they'd be wearing for the next five months. The man across from me took up two seats diagonally, his top half dipped sideways in sleep-skew. I didn't want to read, so I listened to the kind of music I can't listen to while reading. I fell asleep quickly, woke with the word "kite" at the back of my mouth and a sentence about the promise of PhDs in antediluvian sunlight.

TUESDAY

This morning the good-looking couple had suitcases and water bottles; maybe after work they were going to the airport to go somewhere delightful, or maybe they were going on simultaneous business trips. But on the train they were going to the same place, as they always do, and I couldn't remember what stop they get off at every day; my jealousy, it seemed, clouded over any observations that weren't about them being physically near each other, smiling.

WEDNESDAY

My first two years here, I called it the ocean, my boss said of Lake Michigan as we leaned into a cold wind from the east.

THURSDAY

A lawyer read a *New York Times Magazine* story about Kesha. I looked forward to reading the article later. Our coats rustled against each other, raincoat plastic against wool. Everyone, that morning, seemed to have wedding rings.

FRIDAY

My boss caught me reading *The Innovator's Dilemma*, a deeply dull business book, written in the passive voice, with no characters, only companies and numbers and terms italicized to emphasize and give the terms the polish of a foreign-language false cognate. This sentence bothered me: "Rising share prices make stock option plans an inexpensive way to provide incentive to and to reward valuable employees."

THURSDAY

All at once I figured out the metaphor in the Joni Mitchell song "A Case of You," and I was either disappointed or excited. Cubs fans galore.

WEDNESDAY

Was everyone more miserable today? I think so. A teacher cried across from me. I stared out the window, then back at her. Online, I found encouragement and calls for "self-care," a phrase I don't like. Tell me what I should *do*.

WEDNESDAY

The news continued, screen saturation with nearly everyone reading about the hate and disruption. And the rest of us, those who read books, who prefer keeping the small screen dark during the commute, a time for silence, the undoing of cuticles or willful forgetting and soft denial—we waited.

THURSDAY

From the book I'm reading: "Our lives are worth more than the lives of others." Last night Matt told me how traumatized he was by seeing a white man spit on a black woman: Matt chased after him, into the midnight suburban streets and back into the safety of the train station, where transit workers made sure the white man did no physical harm, left him to his racial slurs as he slithered away into the dark.

FRIDAY

My boots chopped at my ankles, and their tongues slipped sideways. My sweater rode up beneath my coat, the bottom edge at bra-level. My nose itched. My hair didn't sit right. My music wouldn't play, and I had to restart my phone over and over. At work, my wrists tilted incorrigibly away from the keyboard. I smelled blood, the iron of winter dryness, the sandpaper whoosh of dry nostrils against dry air. I am often a mouth-breather, and this morning I couldn't keep my lips sealed for the life of me.

TUESDAY

A little girl delighted in words, singing about tuna fish and the word "no." A man delighted in the phone, his headphones cord draped across his face so the microphone rested on his right cheek. His lips crept into a smile. The construction worker to my left leaned into me in the turns; I leaned forward. I had a different bag this morning, no book, and so I read on my phone, grateful for the cloud. And suddenly we were underground, the train having crawled downhill without my noticing. Thick bundles of cords lined the tunnel walls, undulating imperfectly.

THURSDAY

The nice thing about winter is that people wear mittens and gloves—fewer fingers for me to inspect for wedding rings.

FRIDAY

Look at me, being a good Samaritan, I said to myself. This will be a good story to tell, I continued, deepening the narration until I was no longer sure whether I'd actually told the woman her backpack was open, revealing folded twenty-dollar bills and a bottle of Adderall. Nor was I sure I'd said something because I wanted to help her avoid theft or because I'd wanted to become, for the train ride and in its recollection, the type of person who wants to help other people.

FRIDAY

If not the rings then the wrinkles and if not the wrinkles then the hair, and if not the hair then the skin on the backs of hands, the skin on necks, the skin on lips. If not the morning then the evening. If not the father then the husband.

MONDAY

This morning I forced myself to praise the reading I could do, the seat I had, the people on either side of me for staying still and contained. I praised pants with the right elasticity for sitting all day. I praised their thin wale and that it had not yet rubbed away. I praised the lawyers and teachers whose professions I could read in the paperwork on their laps. I praised cell phone service, a generous data plan, streaming everything; I praised the subscription model.

TUESDAY

This morning, a man in layers of green-and-tan camouflage woke with a jerk and immediately reached into his plastic bag of bagels, tore off a piece, chewed, and fell back to sleep in a chin-to-chest hunching. Maybe tonight, I thought, I'll catch the holiday train, which I saw last night at the station; I took photos of Santa Claus and his elves handing out candy canes.

WEDNESDAY

The temperature hovered just below zero, and I was glad to wait only five minutes for my connection. I flipped my hood off as I boarded, left my hat on. Long underwear soothes like freshly shaved legs.

WEDNESDAY

"You are an eternal personality," said the heading in the book the woman next to me was holding. Her hand covered the title, and a dust bunny skipped across the train, caught in the conflicting currents from the door and the under-the-seat heaters. I had decisions to make, and I decided to make them. A bag floated by on cold air. The weather, every morning, is a treat.

MATCH

oogling, I sleuthed after his last name the day of our first date. He was easy to find despite a profile that contained only two words in all caps: "MALE HUMAN." I'd barely had to think of my opening line: Hello, male human. To which he responded, Hello, fellow human. This was somehow enough to decide to meet him at a bar, a date I prepared for with a workday dehydration headache I was too lazy to undo. It was negative degrees outside, and none of my regular date outfits worked. The more dates I went on, the more tempted I was to not dress up at all. If they really like me, I thought, they'll accept me in my second-tier clothes.

But I couldn't follow through, and I wore the same top-tier outfits again and again. It was easiest if a week contained only first dates because I could wear the same thing on all of them and remember to wear that outfit on none of the second dates. Otherwise I'd worry about forgetting what I'd worn with whom.

The male human, it turned out, was named Robert and worked for a brewery up the street from me. But beer is boring, he said. What do you do? But what I do is boring too, I said, and we went back to mourning the loss of a Clinton presidency. He had a beard like all beer men, one that was fluffy and coarse and that made me wonder what his lips looked like naked. Pool balls clinked against each other after skimming soft across felt. This man told me that in times like this we needed community more than ever. We talked about the Cubs win, how happy the city had been compared to how downtrodden it was today, the day after Election Day. There was a difference, of course, between sports and national politics, but all the same, he said, it was about community. I was too sad to agree or disagree. The waiter asked again and again if we wanted more beer until we finally said yes, an implicit agreement that the date was going well enough to at least sign on for whatever portion of an hour it takes to drink a pint. The room had disappeared around us, no other couples at the bar, no people holding both of the glass double doors open so a chill that began in our fingertips settled into our arms and torsos and my bangs blew in the draft. Yet these things happened. These were things that were happening to me.

At some point during every app-enabled date—which is to say, every date I went on—Donald Trump came up. He was easy to talk about, and though he was at first little more than small talk, we tried to avoid mere banter, an attempt at making the dates feel meaningful. As we talked about the horrors of what a Trump presidency might mean, we studied each other. We focused on ourselves. We felt little shame for doing so; dating was our responsibility, and fuck it all if Donald Trump was going to get in the way.

Such was the spirit of online dating: Nothing could stop us, not geographical boundaries, not a bad time the night before, or work the next day, or the threat of fascism. Our responsibility was to meet as many people as possible, to act on the compulsive worry that there might be someone even better out there if only we'd swipe enough to find them.

In between dates, we texted and browsed, brushing away

potential suitors or pulling their faces toward us. I did this on the couch, in between dinner and judo practice. I did not mention this part of my day to my dates, nor when the thumbs on the other end tapped, What are you up to? I pretended I was watching TV, cooking, reading. I tried to project an image of someone cultured but not uptight, independent but not lonely, interested but not desperate. The possibilities felt endless.

We led interesting lives on the apps. We had always just arrived from somewhere—dinner, a bar, work. We were people with hobbies that could be simply listed, jobs summed up in two or three words. We had friends but we tried not to mention them, friends who'd be more plentiful and friendships that would be stronger if we weren't so preoccupied with finding romantic partnership.

Before Donald Trump catalyzed Robert's conversation about building community, there was first the meeting. I worried he wouldn't recognize me bundled up and I wouldn't recognize him through my cold-fogged glasses. Most of the people on the barstools still had their coats on. As we spotted each other, I waved like you wave to a friend leaving in a car, and he said, Rachel? and I said, Yes. He didn't like the way the bar angled, so we moved to a table, where I kept prematurely putting my glasses back on before they'd defrosted. I tasted his beer before ordering my own, and it seemed that I should at least know his last name.

We were at a shitty open-mic night at a shitty bar. A tiny white dog sat at the counter on a barstool, and a drunk man swayed. Stickers peeled from the walls, band names illegible in faded blues and blacks. The hot water pipes, painted brown, were the only source of heat. At the bar I asked twice for a Schlitz, and the third time the bartender leaned toward me, I toward her, as I enunciated that single awkward syllable.

I hadn't known if this was the right place from outside; it had seemed too dark, the neon signs too tired. But maybe it was the new streetlight—a brighter LED model—washing the scene out. Maybe it was my winter coat's fur-edged hood and the resulting lack of peripheral vision playing tricks on me.

The musical duo on stage sang sweetly and tediously about love and lawyers over a plucked electric guitar that was high on reverb and precision. The couple next to us was high, and I was just waiting for the whole thing to end. No matter how hard I tried to pay attention to the people on stage or the hot pipes I'd jammed my chair up against, I thought instead about what it meant that I couldn't pay attention to much of anything. I was out of it, analyzing and predicting, measuring, as it were, the present.

These men I went on dates with brought up online dating unselfconsciously, with an earnestness they wouldn't use in follow-up texts, with a straightforwardness I yearned for. Before the first open-mic performer took the stage, as we sat picking the labels off our beer bottles, Robert said he thought Tinder is democratic, that it introduces people to a cross-section of society they wouldn't usually encounter. I nodded. The silences were awkward but we laughed at each other's jokes and ordered more beers; he paid.

Did I like him more than Matt, whom I'd be going on a second date with later that week? Did we laugh more? Did he share more personal details? Would it be easier to get to know him? Was he better-looking?

Each man was a point of comparison for the others, each date a piece of the rubric, ranked like a middle schooler's homework—needs improvement, satisfactory, good, excellent—all graded on a curve, so the more satisfactory dates there were, the more the good ones would seem excellent. I wanted to share this theory with the table across from us, where four midforties professors discussed the merits of curved grading, deliberating its fairness. Maybe, if my system was airtight, I could make a fair assessment. Or maybe I'd be unable to tell the men apart, each one reduced by the rubric to traits made generic in analysis.

But there on the date with bearded Robert and my fogged glasses, I didn't need to separate the person from his profile because they were, for once, pretty much the same. He looked and dressed as I expected him to—plaid shirt and "relaxed-fit" jeans—and I hoped my profile also fit with the real me. I didn't care whether I was the avatar or the avatar me—I just cared whether they were similar.

Two beers in, Robert asked me if I thought the date was going well. I must have given him a look, because he explained: On a recent date with a woman who was obviously having no fun at all, he'd asked her the same question. She said that no, the date was not going well, so he asked her why she'd agreed to a second drink. She wasn't sure. He gave her permission to leave—which should've been a red flag to me, but I was too busy trying to think of a response that I barely noticed what he was saying.

The apps were a game of catch-up, a race toward a goal that encouraged us to think about next steps rather than what we were currently experiencing, which could be considered meeting people or could be considered—in a word from David Foster Wallace—interfacing.

The first level of interface was the app icon: a flame for Tinder, a beehive for Bumble. Behind them, stacks of virtual playing cards awaited, faces upon faces flung to the side with quick flicks of the thumb, like dealing cards—but to whom and what was the ante? Bumble shaded its texts yellow, Tinder aqua, so though the messages might look at first like regular texts, they were, to anyone giving the screen more than a glance, obviously not. You weren't just texting one friend; you were flirting with several strangers simultaneously, there in public, for anyone to see.

The general mechanics of the two apps were similar, save for one main thing: On heterosexual Bumble, the woman had to talk first, and she had twenty-four hours after matching with someone to do so. It was this requirement that made some consider the app more feminist than Tinder; it was this requirement that took away, for me, the pressure of going first: I *had* to say something—there was no choice.

The most shameful and shameless app I played with was The League. To be accepted, my Facebook and LinkedIn profiles were screened, though I suspected this was a ruse.

I got an email from The League on Thanksgiving chiding me for not using the app enough. "'Inactive' users hurt the match rate and cause our 'active' users to become frustrated," the letter began. Maybe I was on vacation, it suggested, or maybe I was in a new relationship. If this was the case, I could pay to put the app on hold so I could jump right back in, if necessary. The vacation would end; the relationship would run its course. The app depended on it.

If I didn't start using The League again or paying for a hiatus, I'd be kicked out and unable to rejoin without paying a monthly fee. I quickly swiped to the dating screen of my phone and reopened the app. I said no to the four "potential soulmates." They all listed golf as one of their interests.

I'd grown used to certain profiles, categories that were usually made clear in the first photo. There were men who held up large fish; men looking pensive in the driver's seats of cars; men posed with other, look-alike men; men posed with men who were their physical opposites; men playing guitar; men standing next to sexy women; men posed with their moms, with babies, with puppies; men playing sports; shirtless men with American-flag swim trunks; shirtless men on boats; men in the wilderness; men taking selfies in bathroom mirrors.

Surely there were equivalent categories of women, and surely I fell into one of them, which meant that there were men who also categorically rejected women like me.

A prospect might look too Abercrombie-hot for me to say yes; he'd never go for a crewneck-sweater wearer like me, I'd think. But as soon as I'd swipe left, I'd wonder what the harm in swiping the other way would have been. The risk that comes from matching is minimal—or even nonexistent: You never ever even have to say hi. A friend, the person who first convinced me to try app-dating, reminded me of this. The stakes couldn't be lower, he said.

But why clog up the app with false positives? And why make myself feel worse: The more times I swiped right, the more matches I expected to get in return, and when the matches trickled to a halt, the more I thought I'd never find anyone, that I was only wasting time, that the sliver of faith I had in dating apps was ill-advised and delusional.

Trapped with my phone and its programming, I swiped compulsively. I'd slow down a few dates in with the same dude, because there simply weren't enough nights in the week to explore other options. But I knew those other options were still there, and my inactivity, as The League reminded me, wasn't helping anyone.

The second date with Robert was cocktails at a bar, the third was brunch, and the fourth was cocktails at my house. I prepared by vacuuming, wiping the counters with Fantastik, and taking the dishes off the drying rack. Next door, my neighbor paid a food delivery guy; upstairs, a woman walked. Before Robert arrived, I wore my fleece to stay as warm as possible and sat on the couch dragging my fingers across my phone, briefly in one of the dating apps and then more intently in the dots game I crave during downtime and productivity alike, its mindlessness cloaked in a false sense of strategy that feels better—more rational, more purposeful, and therefore more responsible—than the idea of chance or, worse, the reality of it. I had left the dining room light on, which shone beyond and into the living room, where a halogen lamp warmed me from above, its yellow glow dimmed to a level I thought was sufficiently romantic but not threateningly so. When the doorbell rang, I leapt and tore off the fleece and hung it in the closet, out of sight.

It's so—tidy, he said, before even looking at me. We stood across from each other in the living room, on either side of a Persian rug. He started to bend to take his shoes off and I told him he didn't have to, even though he'd left a trail of salt and slush from the door to where he now stood. I led him to the kitchen, asked what he wanted to drink. The space was made narrow by two bodies instead of one, and I had to shuffle sideways past him, bumping the stove handle, to get to the refrigerator, whose moaning had never been more obvious or loud.

I assured him my apartment looked this way was because I'd dropped into a cleaning frenzy yesterday. I didn't want to seem prepared; I wanted to be casual and with the right amount of effort—that is, just enough to suggest potential affection should potential affection ever develop, but definitely not overeager. But why would I be using a dating app if I weren't eager to start a relationship?

This was the question I often asked myself, semideep in the throes of app-dating. It was my first stint on the apps, albeit long enough that "stint" is probably inaccurate: A few weeks turned into a month, the months multiplied, more second and third dates than I should have gone on, and suddenly it'd been a year since I started swiping.

I'd start each night with dinner alone in my apartment. I liked to get dressed for the date before eating, lest the question of what to wear distract me from enjoying my pasta carbonara or big salad or leftover cheeseburger. I'd read the newspaper from the previous Sunday and drink a cocktail made standing next to my sink. No matter what, I couldn't get myself to eat at a leisurely pace, nor could I get myself to show up the few minutes late I thought would make me seem easygoing. But every time I'd try, stalling departure by sitting on my couch, coat on, twiddling around Twitter. In the winter I'd put my purse strap under my hood, and a block from the bar I'd reach behind my head to untangle the strap from the hood and drape the purse over my shoulder so I wouldn't have to perform the awkward maneuver in front of anyone. I'd blow my winter-runny nose and open the bar door, the threshold metaphorically noticeable each time.

In addition to Donald Trump, on those dates we talked about

pizza and tacos and beer. We asked about TV shows and books, college and cities we'd lived in, picking up where we'd left off on the apps, where we'd presented only uncomplicated and tangible facts: place of residence, job, what music we were listening to. We steeped in each other's data. And every time a conversation fizzled and flirtation came to a halt, I would remember that were I actually with someone else, not sitting there with a stranger or, afterward, alone, I'd be distracted not by the promise of data-driven answers to precise and emotionless questions but instead by the messiness of another person.

The night after Robert came over, I went out with Thomas, a playwright. We met in front of the bar we'd chosen, found it closed, and ended up at a tacky Italian restaurant with linty white tablecloths and menus the size of newspapers. We sat on tall chairs and drank sweet drinks. These were the only details I remembered on the train ride home. Had I been so nervous that I was unable to absorb the facts of the evening? Or was I too busy reminding myself that the date was going well? The whole thing had felt a bit like video-chatting: You pretend you're looking at the other person when really you're watching yourself. And even if you were looking at each other, there's no way you'd ever make true eye contact and know it, because to do so, you'd both need to look into the tiny cameras on the top edge of your screens, and you wouldn't see each other seeing each other.

It was like the month when I tracked my steps with a watch, how I'd think of the tracking as I was walking instead of falling into the meditative state walking inspires. Then, everything I passed would remind me of something I needed to do: the music store (I should set aside more time to play guitar), the bank (I should start buying Christmas presents soon), the Starbucks (I should text my friend who used to work there), the crosswalks (I'm supposed to be thinking about walking but am instead thinking about thinking about walking). The wind would fight through leafless trees as I'd pass those places and worry those worries.

Everyone's always saying it's a journey, everything's a journey, but they're also saying it's important to have goals. I've never convinced myself that getting there is as important as having arrived, that the journey, as they say, is worth more than the destination. Counting steps reinforced this idea, but it did it in a tricky way: by making the journey itself a goal, each step a success, achieved because it was enumerated, made valuable by its newfound tangibility, the fact of it recorded. Or, each date an achievement made valuable by its structured setup, loneliness ignored.

The things we stop noticing on walks: limps and swinging arms, storefronts, cracks in the sidewalk, streetlights. And on dates: the pants he's wearing, how many siblings he has, the brightness of the bar. But never solitude—that remained, barely smudged by the presence of Robert and Thomas and Matt and Chase and the other Chase and everyone else.

The greater the number of dates, the more I adjusted to them, and the lonelier I felt. Each new face was an indication that the others hadn't gone well. More matches were an indication that all of the other matches didn't pan out. I saw not possibility but hopelessness.

Even when I stopped tracking, I couldn't walk without thinking about the walk, without needing the walk to have a purpose. I realized I'd always been that way; tracking only made it more obvious. Step-counting wasn't distracting me, exactly. My need to be productive was only another distraction, because at the heart of my worry was a single concern: I'd always be lonely.

Robert and I scheduled our next date. The hour before, I put on fresh eyeliner and my date shirt, negroni on the table, and paused at the sound of my phone. Could we reschedule? he texted. I wanted to pick apart the timing: Was it really at the moment his phone died that he decided he was too tired to hang out? So I didn't seem overbearing, I waited a few minutes before saying anything, then— Sure, fine. And I opened Tinder, the saddest consolation: When one dude doesn't work out, replace him—or the promise of him— with another from among the infinitude of others. This was what it had come to: searching for familiarity in strangers, comparisons of potentials to already-hads, as if these things could be measured out in advance, as if doing so wouldn't just remind me that those relationships were long gone. I was too wrapped up in analysis and prediction to actually notice I wasn't feeling anything at all about these interactions.

I sat there in my date outfit, hoping Robert would write back, not knowing he'd ghost completely a few days later. I waited for a new match to come up and counted previous matches to make myself feel likable. Clocks ticked, the radiators hissed awake, the phone chimed—a new match, a fresh conversation. As we chatted about books, I couldn't let go of the hope that the internet, in its plenitude of binaries and data, held the answer.

The chemical engineer replaced the computer programmer, who replaced the playwright, who canceled out the beer dude. Stephen tried convincing me that a three-dollar shot of whiskey would make me feel more awake, Aaron tried to share an Uber home, assuring me he'd pay me back with a drink next time. Ben's thick baritone masked relentlessly tedious conversation. Mike was a weightlifter. We drank beer and whiskey and wine. There was the same outfit, over and over.

I found false equivalence in etymology: "Date" and "data" both come from the same Latin, *dare*, for "give."

The dates gave me hope and anxiety, blisters on my heels at night and mascara circles under my eyes in the morning, ATM fees and empty beer bottles. The apps offered human data, potential companionship. In the end, the given was solitude, exactly what I'd started with.

EXCHANGE

I never lie at Bed Bath & Beyond. This toothbrush stopped vibrating. This hair dryer caught on fire. This comforter is no longer puffy. This Cuisinart shot out smoke. These sheets got small in the wash. I am not a good liar, only a good editor. There are rarely follow-up questions.

The electric toothbrush was the most recent in a series of successful, self-edifying exchanges made at Bed Bath & Beyond, a store whose Beyond, I like to think, refers to its liberal return policy on top of its already paradisiacal domestic promise of having finally made it to adulthood. The toothbrush broke over months of me knocking it off its charger, precariously balanced between a towel bar and the wall; my bathroom had no counter or power outlets, so my toothbrush sat as far as its cord stretched, woven through a notch in the door threshold to the nearest outlet in the other room, where it burst forth in a tangle of too many cords like the hair of a cartoon who's stuck her finger into a light socket.

The final blow came on the third and last night of a fling with a man who liked whiskey and J. D. Salinger. It had seemed promising the first night and doomed by the second. As I tried to fall asleep before the man came back in from the bathroom, I heard the familiar crash of electric toothbrush against tile. The sound reminded me, as always, of the foreboding plastic crack a TI-83 Plus calculator makes when it slides off a desk onto a thinly carpeted floor, a sound that would make my high school calculus teacher say, every time, his beard framing a curmudgeon's grimace, That's not a very good thing to do to a calculator.

An hour after the crash, after brushing my teeth the normal, old-fashioned way, the man was asleep, and I wanted him to leave. I wanted it to be tomorrow, when I'd go to Bed Bath & Beyond to get a new toothbrush.

I had not bought this Philips Sonicare DiamondClean Rechargeable Electric Toothbrush in White; it came courtesy of Philips' PR department, which wanted me to review it for the tech magazine I used to work for. It was one of many perks of the job, the primary being the job itself—the people, the work, and the fact that it existed: A few months before the toothbrush landed on my desk, the hostile machismo at the job I'd come to New York for became intolerable, and I quit. I gave myself three days for wallowing. Then I went to a Midtown Aldo and bought my first pair of heels and learned to wobble in them, wearing them only as long as each interview lasted and changing out of them while leaning against buildings. I went to the News Corp. building and the Condé Nast Building and the Hearst Tower and, the day after I got the new job, to the Bed Bath & Beyond on the cusp of where the Financial District becomes Tribeca. I had decided weeks before that I would reward myself for getting hired, for writing ten or twenty or thirty polite cover letters (the embarrassing self-promotion, the stilted language of "skills" and "I welcome the opportunity") and pretending to want jobs I didn't by smiling and asking follow-up questions—and that the reward would be a new comforter, something that would fit the queen-size bed I planned to get one day, after leaving New York.

I'd done my research. The Wamsutta Cool and Fresh Down Alternative Comforter was just for me: fake feathers, to avoid allergy-induced congestion, in a thickness and arrangement that would supposedly lessen my night sweats. After I left the tech-magazine job for grad school in the middle of the country, I learned that neither of those things was necessary: It turns out my childhood down allergy had subsided, and my night sweats were a side effect of the antidepressants I was taking, not of my bedspread.

I learned too, via firsthand experience and reviews on the Bed Bath & Beyond website (and some Amazon reviews for validation) that down-alternative fillings tend to bunch up, leaving wide expanses of sheet-thin fabric interrupted by sudden lumps, a topography not unlike that of the Upper Midwest. So of course that first grad-school spring, when life was no longer novel, just different, I headed out for an exchange at the nearby Bed Bath & Beyond, conveniently located not next to a Whole Foods, like the one I went to in New York, or a Trader Joe's, like the one I went to growing up in Chicago, but next to I-80. Inside, they're all beautifully the same. No regional distinctions change layout: Kitchen gadgets are always to the right when you walk in, bath stuff to the left, picture frames in the middle, and SodaStream accessories throughout. There's a certain comfort to be found rounding the store's racetrack aisles, when just buying a new shower curtain feels like taking control of your life, the implied declaration that you'll get a handle on all your shit, be productive, be happy. It's the certain comfort of the domestic possibility I learned from my mother and that first promising exchange, sans receipt or packaging, when I was ten or twelve, of the best toaster either of us has ever used.

The man at the customer service desk in the I-80-adjacent Bed Bath & Beyond hardly peeked inside the bag I'd stuffed the comforter into; he didn't notice or didn't want to mention the drool stains; he said, Go pick out a new one. My new one is filled with real feathers and was cheaper than the original; using my credit I bought some toothbrush heads, 20 percent off with an expired coupon.

This was pure fantasy—but in real life! The dream of ergonomic spatulas and finely gridded cheese graters and other unnecessary (but necessary) kitchen gadgets I let myself indulge in once, twice a year max. Hence the exchanges, which feel so close to actual purchases but require no extra money, just a half hour or so to give me the illusion of being the kind of person who can buy a new Cuisinart once a year—the kind of person who calls such a purchase frugal because it was made with a coupon. Does it count as conspicuous consumption if I need that Cuisinart because I like to make pesto and I like to make pesto because the mindless process of it, like very few things, makes me happy? That cooking in general is one of the very few things that makes me happy? With that kind of justification, Bed Bath & Beyond became not just normal but crucial.

The beauty of living this way is that the objects are simultaneously temporary—they can be exchanged often—and permanent—they can be exchanged infinitely, each time for a replacement so indistinguishable from the original that often I'll forget how many times I've exchanged a thing and, eventually, that I've exchanged it at all. Replacements can happen forever, stretching into a future when I'll swap the old for new just to keep things the same. I never have to say goodbye; my fantasy life accumulates. And so does the illusion of permanence in my life—that I've reached a stage when I can stay put. Of course that's not true. Of course there's a Bed Bath & Beyond in every state.

But I did not buy this toothbrush at a Bed Bath & Beyond in any state. I now lived in a place where I said "run errands" and I ran them in a car. It was my second winter in the middle of nowhere. Still, I had hope. I put the toothbrush in what little packaging I had, coiling the charging cable and securing it with a twist tie—it looks real this way, I thought—and drove toward the highway, where, merging, I caught a glimpse of myself reflected in the salty windshield and saw the face of a grown-up. I still was not lying at Bed Bath & Beyond, but the omissions were getting larger. The store had become a place of aspirational exchanging, not aspirational buying, the hope for a better future replaced by the hope for one that's exactly the same. It's an unacceptable hope, but what else to do besides pretend and hold onto the receipt.

There was no problem returning the toothbrush. I waited in line for what felt like too long but only in the deeply selfish way that standing in line for something you don't deserve feels too long the moment you start doing it. I handed the customer-service man the toothbrush case, toothbrush nestled inside, and the charger, and told him about the vibration problem. Someone else brought me a new toothbrush from the storeroom, and I left. No one ever checked to make sure the toothbrush was actually in the case.

I marched out into the anonymous parking lot proud and jubilant. I told myself, as I do after every Bed Bath & Beyond trip, not just the exchanges, how responsible an object owner I am, how responsible a consumer! I am the type of person who takes action when there's something wrong. I act promptly. I speak politely yet firmly with the people at customer service. I even smile and make eye contact when I say thank you. I dress, sometimes, like a real adult.

SUBMISSION

There's no way to argue that cauliflower ears are feminine. Crunched cartilage swells into permanent lumps that turn the ears' gentle curves into thick fleshy pucks. They jut from the head; they look good on no one, especially not on women, and especially not on women who make their living giving other women cauliflower ears for money while looking sexy.

Cauliflower ears are common in Buffalo Wild Wings, the haven of, among other things, pay-per-view mixed martial arts fights. They were common on the winter night when I and three friends pretended to be ironically eating chicken wings and watching MMA on TV when really we were doing both in earnest. We were there to watch the fight between "Rowdy" Ronda Rousey, the reigning Ultimate Fighting Championship bantamweight champion, and "Alpha" Cat Zingano. Like me, Ronda grew up doing judo. Unlike me, Ronda made it far past number four in the US senior rankings, hitting number one, winning tons, including a bronze medal at the Olympics. Then she turned into a cage-fighting superstar.

That night, Ronda seemed to be wearing two bras. Cat wore a skintight tank top. Both toed the line of what's an acceptable display of femininity; neither had cauliflower ears. Images of the two flashed on-screen between the men's fights—a tease held in staged photos, their noses nearly touching, fists up—punctuated by clips of them beating up other women.

I could really get into this, I told my friends many times that night. I meant being a spectator. Performing—not to mention getting hit in the face and parading around in underwear—would be too much. Over two decades of doing judo, I had never been able to fully convince myself that fighting was a performance, at least in part. But what else to call the reason some women wear makeup to practice and others put their names in pink stitching on their black belts? We've been taught, after all, that to be an athletic woman you still have to be a woman, and to work through the logical difficulty that men are muscular and women are not, you have to change something; so the change comes from our muscles, which we're supposed to call feminine, as if to say we have the muscles because we're women, not in spite of it. But to ask for a definition that doesn't rely on the body alone—that'd be too risky, too close to letting women shrug off the responsibility of always reminding the world that we're women.

The men who fought before Ronda were boring but beautiful, and my friends and I justified our objectifying ogling by telling each other, It's fine, there's wage inequality. Women as the main fight—a win for feminism, we told ourselves. But it was almost a backhanded one, so obviously driven by the male gaze, that tired yet apt description of looking: The men in Buffalo Wild Wings want to be the men they watch on TV; they want to fuck the women.

We spent those opening fights eating wings that were disappointingly boneless, that is, not wings but gussied-up chicken breasts, a weak replacement partly in response to the country's ongoing wing shortage and partly a capitulation to those afraid of bones and gnawing on them—the people who really shouldn't be eating meat in the first place.

But the wings were good. We ate them through the first fight and the second, took a break during the third, and then we were drunk, so we ate them through the fourth, the glistening skin leaving sticky patches on our cheeks that we removed using individually wrapped moist towelettes, a term so appropriate for an evening of waiting to watch nearly naked adult women dripping in blood and sweat (and yes, in the end, tears too) in a room of sticky-faced men drinking wheat beer.

Ronda and Cat appeared on screen. They spent the prefight minutes jiggling and jumping on their sides of the octagon, lips wrapped around mouthguards that turned their faces unavoidably vicious. Stats flashed on-screen, pitting the fighters against each other in comfortably objective numbers—height, weight, win-loss record. The two women shifted back and forth in their stances, hardly blinked. Their faces shone with Vaseline.

The TVs in Buffalo Wild Wings were, by Ronda's fight, all playing the same thing. My friends and I still had some so-called wings left. I ordered another whiskey and could tell my memories were thinning but couldn't tell whether it was the existential unease of the fight narrowing inward that made me unable to take in what was happening around me—the physical facts of the story—or that I was actually close to blacking out.

So many TVs, each with a slightly different color calibration, one that put Ronda's red cheeks in stark relief against Cat's white shirt, another that washed everyone out into flat shapes, cardboard cutouts of fighters, a double remove—so many TVs that the four of us watching all faced different ways, either surrounded into communal viewing, chicken wings and booze and khaki-and-button-up-clad dudes collapsing us into one, or cut apart by angles into people talking at each other and no one listening, all swept into ourselves by drinking and watching, left with only the buzzing awareness that this was actually happening. We were pummeled into trusting the importance of this thing which really was just another sport, a bizarre display of money and bodies masquerading as narrative.

The fight ended in fourteen seconds. The two neared each other, Ronda with her left foot forward, Cat with her right, and Cat took that right foot and tried to hit Ronda with it, but Ronda moved to the side and hugged Cat, who seemed to be throwing Ronda to the ground, who seemed to be in control as Ronda landed head first with legs kicking the air but the shift was subtle and then it was Cat flipping over her own head and with an arm caught in Ronda's and then an arm pried the wrong way; a tapout, over.

Ronda ripped out her mouthguard and bounced around as her entourage crowded onto the mat. They were joined by commentator Joe Rogan, whose shaved head glistened in the spotlight and wrinkled when he moved his mouth, as if there were worms under his skin. Ronda and her dudes wore all black, each with a pair of giant red headphones around their necks, Ronda with a can of Monster. "I can't wait to get some hot wings right now, Joe," she said. Her hand was on his shoulder and they were both beaming.

Our hands in Buffalo Wild Wings were in the air; we cheered and looked at each other, beaming too. One friend was crying. Did you see that? we asked uselessly. Did you see it?—we meant the armbar, but also that sharp ferocity tying the fighters together, fighters who were bodies and who were, therefore, unafraid of anything except an ending. It came on quick, this sudden arousal, and only after would I realize that like any other pleasure, the problem was as soon as I felt it, it was over.

Cat waited for her turn outside of the octagon, where Joe Rogan put his hand on her shoulder, thumb hovering above it, thumb admitting what the rest of his body wouldn't—that he didn't really want to be touching a sweaty loser. He told her: "This is obviously a very disappointing moment for you—give us your thoughts on what just happened and what your strategy was going into this fight." Cat paused, shook her head slowly, looked down, kept looking down, and said, finally: "I want to do it again. I just—fuck." Then Joe Rogan asked Cat to recount what happened in those fourteen seconds, and she did, because this is part of the fighting contract— that you'll face your fuck-ups as soon as you've finished fucking up. That wasn't enough for Joe Rogan; he wanted an explanation for why she lost, as if the fight itself hadn't given him a good enough answer. He wanted self-confident blather, simultaneously the fuel and the substance of fight interviews, the thing that turns men into shit-talkers and women into bitches. But Cat would be neither: "She did it—she fucking won! She did it! She did good!" and she's clapping her mitted hands, looking up for the first time: "That was a good armbar! She did it!"

So what was there left to do? the MMA world wondered. Do what every sport does to the women who are better than all other women: Make them compete against men. But Ronda said no, that letting a man hit a woman on TV would be "a bad image to put across," and I still can't decide whether that's a feminist reaction to sexism or a savvy sidestep around the implication that how women compare to men is still the real measure of success—as if to gauge how good Ronda is, you must put her in the octagon with a man, and to gauge her as a woman, you must do the same. The men watching can't—or refuse to—understand otherwise; the men watching want the familiar, and so the men watching find comfort in UFC president Dana White's substitution: Ronda is "like a fucking dude trapped in this beautiful body."

Boys will be boys, and women will be bitches—unless they become boys. But they never will, no matter what Dana White or anyone else says, especially when they're in octagonal rings wearing bras specifically designed to reveal cleavage and provide athletic support in equal measure. Ronda is not a woman in a man's body, and that makes her all the more dangerous. It's when women threaten to take attention from men with their own tools—here, fighting—but without the men themselves that the men feel truly threatened; they see these women turning what once was called masculine into something neither masculine nor feminine, just good.

YARDSTICK

Before women were all hunched over screens, applying filters and tapping out hashtags to food photos, we were hunched over sinks, sudsing dishes and keeping an eye on the stove. Today's kitchens may have more machines, but they remain abuzz with structured and artificial femininity, from white aprons to pink KitchenAids. Everything matches, even the woman, whose body the kitchen has been designed to fit—albeit inaccurately—since almost a century ago, when engineers measured thousands of women to try to make housework more comfortable.

Over the last one hundred years, kitchens have grown, walls have fallen, and appliances have multiplied, but the kitchen protagonist—a woman, standardized—has stayed the same. So has the height of the countertops, sink, and oven.

Until the 1930s, kitchen-surface heights, like clothing, varied as people did, with kitchens and clothes matching the women in them, rather than the other way around. Engineers even sought to bring precision to the task. Kitchen work would be less backbreaking, they said, if the counters and sinks were the right height for the women using them.

One of those engineers, Christine Frederick, studied women at work to create a chart pairing work-surface height with woman height;

a five-foot-four woman, for instance, would be most comfortable with her countertops and the bottom of her sink 30 inches from the floor. Correct heights, combined with efficient kitchen layouts, could make cooking slightly less of a burden, she wrote.

But American industry, for the sake of more efficient production, needed (and still needs) standards. Two decades after Frederick created her chart, standardization took over. The tailor-made kitchen was gone. While it's easy enough to make adjustable chairs and bikes, it's much harder to build customization into an entire room filled with chunks of wood and granite wedged between heavy, expensive, factory-made appliances.

That didn't bode well for the woman for whom this new, uniformly sized kitchen was being designed and made. The sink was the first kitchen object to be standardized. It became part of the continuous countertop—a single height dipping or lifting for no appliance, a look that fell in line perfectly with modernism's minimalist lines. Everything else rose to meet the lip of the sink— the counters, the stove, the cabinets all converging at 36 inches above the floor, writes Leslie Land in her study of modernism and kitchens. That was much too high for the five-foot-four average-height woman of the time (and of today).

Maybe that height was chosen because it was good for marketing, putting everything an ad-friendly yardstick off the floor. Maybe it was because, as Land writes, another engineer, Lillian Gilbreth, had a five-foot-seven woman in mind when she designed demonstration kitchens with their layouts based on motion studies of women at work; for such a woman, a 31.5-inch sink base, about 5 inches below the sink lip and counters, was ideal. Maybe it was arbitrary. No matter—it was set, giving society that yardstick by which to measure the woman and her space alike. In ads, you can see her in a floral, white-collared dress standing next to her sink, appliance-installation man in overalls and on bent knee holding a ruler and looking up longingly.

These new kitchens may have looked different, but they posed the same dilemma: They were either a way to make unavoidable work less onerous, furnished with objects that supposedly fit women specifically, or a way to make sure the kitchen was fit for only women, specifically. Was the new kitchen a realistic response to the existing societal structures that held women in kitchens? Or did it end up reinforcing sexism by pronouncing the kitchen a space made singularly to fit women's bodies?

Today, our kitchens still have 36-inch everything, and they still have women in them, mostly; in heterosexual couples in the United States, women cook 78 percent of home meals and buy 93 percent of the food. And though we eat fewer home-cooked meals and more commercially prepared foods, the ads for kitchen products still feature, for the most part, stereotypically nurturing women, smiling mothers whose primary concern is caring for their families and who, in their caricatures—in loose-fitting, unthreatening khakis—stand for a commercialized version of the modern woman: someone who is productive but still feminine.

Recently I made gazpacho, which is not cooking but chopping and blending. I made it in the part of my living room I call "kitchen," despite its carpet and obvious placement in the northeast corner of my living room. The tomatoes I used weren't red enough; the photos wouldn't capture the delicious flavor. But they smoothed beautifully in my grandmother's Cuisinart, a machine my mom promised I could have when I moved into my first apartment. We agreed the college apartment didn't count, but the college apartment was where someone turned me on to the still mind-blowing fact that "Cuisinart" is a portmanteau of "cuisine" and "art," which made me question, my mind then expanded, the notion that that apartment somehow wasn't real: If I knew about the wondrous portmanteau, and I knew about the device itself, and I knew about both in an apartment, who cared that it was an apartment owned by the university? The question went unanswered: I was too busy celebrating pre-adulthood that year to pursue the issue of when a space is valid enough to house the most valid of kitchen machines.

Then I moved to Brooklyn, then to a different neighborhood in Brooklyn, to the place in which I'd live for three years with the same two roommates. One cooked; one didn't. I asked my mom again for the Cuisinart. When you live in a real apartment, she said again. I can see now what was happening, and could then too, but why get into the pathos of it when there was a more pressing and tangible issue at hand: I wanted that Cuisinart.

I learned to want in Water Tower Place, Chicago's version of a mall, with the Cuisinart grandmother; I learned in the kitchen, with my mom; and in Bed Bath & Beyond, with my mom and then alone; I learned in magazines and on TV and the internet, where KitchenAids gleamed sophistication and dinner parties. I learned to lust when I learned about the extra Cuisinart in my parents' basement. Sometimes I think I let the lust build subconsciously, as a way to make living on my own less unpleasant, as a way to pretend and convince myself that being an adult wasn't just being lonely and productive—that conspicuous consumption was what saved everyone from loneliness and that productivity was what enabled both.

In the kitchen, the private workplace, I could want and have and produce in a single space. I could be alone yet somehow not feel lonely. I could wear an apron, expertly tied behind my back, and use a cookbook and rubber spatula and somehow not feel like a staid, conformist antifeminist. Intent fades away at some point, but surely not in the kitchen, that domestic Eden so wonderful because of its domesticity, because of its push to produce something whose only purpose, if you're rich enough, is to be consumed, even if first that consumption takes place online, on Instagram and Pinterest, where the goal is objectification and where ongoing experience is translated into the stable present.

I posted a video of the Cuisinart in action to Twitter as soon as I had it. I took the base, bowl, and lid with me on the plane after a Christmas home; my mom mailed me the blade because you still couldn't bring sharp things on airplanes.

The Cuisinart's off-white base and age-tinted once-clear bowl fit in with the dim, fanless stuffiness of my tiny kitchen. There, like in all kitchens, there was no space for worry. Nor is there space for worry in my fantasy kitchen, with its two ovens, six burners, drawers that draw themselves the last 2 inches closed. I aspire to having this kitchen so much sometimes that I wonder if all other aspirations—career success and accolades, a husband who loves me and whom I love—are just aspirations in service of the single true goal: a perfect kitchen in which labor is fun and the burden of production is an opportunity for consumption.

I made gazpacho instead of having dinner with the man who was probably my boyfriend. I wanted to be alone, because with someone else, especially him, domestic fantasy would have been, that night, too close to reality, the refrigerator suddenly with two people's preferred cheeses, femininity entrenched in divided responsibilities. That's not true, though. None of that would have happened were I with him, making gazpacho in the kitchen part of my living room, staring at the plaster wall's cracks lit from the windows behind me by a pink and purple sunset. The space wouldn't have demanded it. I might have, though. Because the fact is I genuinely wanted those things and still do, and even if I'm not sure where the want came from, I'm sure of it. I'm sure of it even though, like the modernist kitchen, the desire was based on standardized measurements meant to stabilize me, to hold me in the domestic story, hunched over or over- and underreaching everywhere but the sink.

That sink is a painted-white metal basin that's old enough to have two handles, one for hot and one for cold, but new enough to have just one faucet. The cabinets, metal too, are coated in contact paper that looks like it belongs in a church basement. The refrigerator is new, about a year old; it replaced an identical one after I complained to my landlord about a sound that made me worry about the fate of my frozen fresh pasta and bagels. The exhaust fan spins clunkily when I flip the switch but it never really gets going; instead of fixing it, I open the windows and put the smoke detector in the refrigerator.

To make up for a complete lack of counter space—there is literally no countertop—I use a dry sink, the same one my parents used as a changing table when I was a baby. It's nearly the perfect height (33 inches) and has room inside for all my pots and pans, my waffle maker, my extra knives, boxes for my coffee grinder and French press, the KitchenAid pasta attachment. The wide door creaks closed and open, revealing, toward the back, a handful of wires my grandfather strung through the belly of the thing to link stereo innards to speakers on the outside. It's the ultimate piece of domestic-perfection furniture, infinitely and indefinitely manipulated, in different houses and states and for different people, each time for the same general purpose: to stand in for a specific missing object. In that sense, it's the opposite of most kitchen furniture, which serves particular purposes—stove for cooking in pots and pans, fridge for keeping food (and smoke detectors) cold, &c.

But no matter how particular the purpose, the shapes are still standard. As is the shape of the woman: By standardizing the kitchen, designers also standardized women's bodies, creating a space in which only a person with a specific body shape could be comfortable.

As continuous countertops filled American kitchens, clothing sizes were being standardized for the first time too. Before the Mail Order Association of America requested a study of women's bodies to create standards, clothing sizes for women were based on bust alone, as men's clothes had been since soldiers' uniforms became uniform in the 1800s. The association wanted simple yet accurate sizes because it wanted fewer returns; sizes, then, were a way to make selling things more efficient.

The first step was figuring out what metrics to base the sizes on. Running off Works Progress Administration funds, two statisticians led a nationwide survey of women's bodies. Their team of one hundred surveyors, dispersed across seven states, collected measurements from nearly fifteen thousand women, all of them white. They used tools like protractors and calipers, as well as a "measuring costume" (shorts and a bra), to get numbers for "hip height," "crotch length," "elbow girth," and fifty-six others.

The results overwhelmed in their refusal to generate uniformity.

Differences in women's bodies cannot, the statisticians wrote, "be described completely by one or even a few measurements, since women do not yield to so simple a classification." So the statisticians settled, coming up with a system based on height and weight, and then settled again—since, they thought, women wouldn't want to provide their weight—and replaced weight with girth. But there were still too many sizes to be practical. In stepped the National Bureau of Standards, which found, somewhere in the data, the foundation for a simpler system: Sizes would come from the bust.

All that measuring, and sizes were still based on the breasts, with an extrapolated hourglass figure filling out the rest of the garment. The idea of the perfect body was sewn right into the clothes.

There have always been beauty standards, but it wasn't until the twentieth century that those standards, like the kitchen, became integrated with uniform measurements. The problem is the standardizers got it wrong; with designs based on simplified ideals, not reality, women became misfits in their own kitchens and clothes alike.

The solution, then, must be the opposite of uniformity: customization. The best way to fit everyone, like the best way to make kitchens more comfortable, is to make objects tailored to individual bodies, rather than tailored to the idea of an individual body. Perhaps we should follow the DIY craze, with its jam-making and pickling, its hand-knitted sweaters and backyard-raised chickens; perhaps we should travel back in time a hundred years, moving perversely against the expansion of women's rights (but keeping those rights all the same), to a time when each kitchen was made for the person within it and each shirt for the person inside.

STARS

T he wall yelled around 3:00 a.m. It gave a hoarse shout, then another and another, like growls through clenched teeth, the throat dried by either volume or winter.

What the fuck was that? my boyfriend whispered. He wasn't supposed to be there; I hadn't told the host. I felt paralyzed, like the wall actually was yelling and was, therefore, an intruder, someone who wouldn't see me if I didn't see him.

The wall kept yelling. Whoever was ringing the clanging metal doorbell was insistent. And drunk, I told my boyfriend—it must be a drunk person who got locked out.

It was Saturday-night-turned-Sunday-morning in an Airbnb apartment, five hours north of our houses. We were there so I could do research, and so we could eat good food. We'd arrived the day before, late afternoon. Behind the tree- and Honda Civic–lined street was an unevenly paved alley, and in that alley were rows of open-air garages, and in one of them, a forearm's circumference off the ground, was a tiny crack, and in it, a black velvet pouch with a set of keys.

In the third-floor apartment, sunlight came from everywhere, and a wooden-slab kitchen island beckoned with a gift basket's wine and toiletries. We went out for dinner, walked too far, and came back to collapse on the white-duvet–covered bed. Why leave guests a white duvet cover? Why invite dirt with cleanliness? The radiator ticked in the corner, a smoke alarm flashed green above it, and I hesitated to put my tote bag anywhere but the hardwood floor and certainly not on the couch, also white. How much a host might want to know about her guests I wasn't sure, but I doubted whatever accidental smudges I might scar that duvet with were the type of information she'd be interested in.

I write to you from my apartment, game day, the drone of marching-band school spirit carried across the river and through my thin windows, no footsteps above yet but they'll come, I'm sure, as I lie down to take a nap. This apartment would be fine for Airbnb, but I wouldn't be; I'd have to hide too many things and actively ignore the suspicion, the expectation, that a hiding place isn't the same as no place at all. That is, my cast-iron skillet, my nonstick frying pan, my guitar—these things would still be in my apartment, just out of sight.

Snooping in the Airbnb apartment was tempting but impossible: I might dislodge a carefully placed hair, I might spill, I might find something I didn't want to know about—I might humanize the persona on the other side of the emails and texts, and I might, then, feel strange sleeping in her bed.

She'd been chipper in her emails—"Can't wait for you to experience Minneapolis!"—and didn't seem the paranoid type, but what did I know? I wondered if she'd hidden a camera somewhere. Even if she hadn't, I was still being watched, in a way, by the prospect of a post-stay rating (both the Airbnb guest and host review each other). I could not think about this while getting ready for bed, standing in front of a lazily dripping faucet, putting in my nightguard. I could not think about it while using the host's dishes, opening kitchen drawers to find the bottle opener. But I could think of nothing else, especially with a boyfriend there not mentioned in the "number of guests" section. Was I being respectful, then, because I'm respectful, or because I might get caught in a lie?

In between doorbell shrieks, we fought with the bed. It was so saggy; we kept rolling into each other, meeting in the middle. That had happened the only other time I stayed at a stranger's house, when my mom and I went to the Newport Folk Festival and spent two nights at the house of a friend of a friend. In the bedroom, on the top floor, was an air mattress unlike any I'd seen. It was an entire air bed, its height the height of a real bed with a mattress atop a box spring, as if this bulbous hunk of black vinyl pumped into the general likeness of a bed could pass for the real thing based on vague shape alone. My mom and I spent most of the night awake and rolling away from each other after the sagginess drew us, again and again, to the center, where we'd touch, sweaty, push off each other to roll back to the sides, loglike. This went on until morning, when streetlights' hint of daytime gave way to the real thing.

I have to warn you, my mom said, coming back up from downstairs, there's a man on the couch.

Indeed there was: a man with a Budweiser bottle next to him, wearing baggy jeans and a blue Johnson & Wales sweatshirt, mouth open. He wasn't there when we got back from the festival the night before. He didn't wake up when my mom, grossed out by the buildup of hair and mildew, scoured the tub.

Was this guy the house owner? We never found out. We knew

little about the owner, only that he was a chef and worked odd hours that would, he said, make it so our time in his house probably wouldn't overlap.

That evening we sat under an umbrella on the rooftop and drank beer next to a pot of tiny marijuana plants. Again we spent the night sliding and rolling, and in the morning, no man on the couch, we left a thank-you note and bottle of wine and boarded the bus to Providence.

The doorbell kept rattling metal on metal for what felt like a half hour but might've just been a few minutes; in the middle of the night all sound feels louder and lengthier than it really is. I imagined this poor drunk slumped against the apartment building's front door, a hand raised, smashing the doorbells, hoping. He'd end up sleeping against the door, I thought, which would wake him on its first inward swing of the morning, when someone with a dog would leave at the hour only people with dogs are out, when there's dew on shrubs and windshields and the clarity of the air feels sharp.

My boyfriend didn't want to let the person in to prove a point. I didn't because he might be a bad guy. At least we agreed on not opening the door. But that made the person keep trying, spending a moment with each doorbell and then moving next door, the muted clanging still strong enough to vibrate through the beams and into our apartment.

How quickly we'd made the place our own, even in words. That night I dreamed there were actually two beds but the other, draped in gold pillows, was decorative only, so we were still stuck on our broken platform. The next day, when my boyfriend met me for lunch, he said he'd partially fixed the bed: The boxspring and mattress were now aligned, though the boxspring was still split down the center. Good, I thought, look how handy my boyfriend is, fixing our bed like that. But it was not our bed, and maybe the host liked it off-kilter. Maybe she'd be upset we took such liberty. Maybe she'd rate me poorly.

By Sunday, we'd lapsed into careless guests. We threw clothes on the floor, we didn't wash our glasses right away, we used the Q-tips in the medicine cabinet. An academic might call our behavior up until that point performative: a careful acting-out of being a houseguest on a houseguest reality TV show. I'd call it normal: another offshoot of everything-is-judged daily life.

Reading on the bed, I looked up as my boyfriend stepped out of the bathroom, a piece of off-white shower curtain in his hand.

I wanted to look out the window, he said, pointing to the shower's street-facing window whose curtain now had a hand-sized hole in it.

In the bathroom, where I stretched my arms against the curtain to get its dimensions, I peered through the hole. Outside was crisp, foreign. A woman walked with purpose to a car, balanced a coffee mug on the roof as she fished keys out of a cavernous tote bag. I searched for shower curtains on Amazon on my phone and found a suitable replacement. The reviews were reassuring: I liked knowing what to expect, but I also liked reading about these people and their bathrooms, their mildew problems and their soap suds.

I never rate anything on Amazon; I find the prospect of winnowing down an object into a certain number of stars daunting. That was the case for Netflix users too for a while; the company got rid of half stars in movie ratings (and then got rid of stars altogether, replacing them with thumbs up and thumbs down) because people were overwhelmed by the choices. Unable to pick from among eleven possible ratings, people stopped picking anything. They couldn't enjoy the twenty-first-century postmovie tradition, couldn't, with such uncertainty, even enjoy the movies they just watched. The point of rating a movie, it turns out, isn't saying how good it was so other people will know. The point is describing yourself, validating that what you just did (watched a movie) was worth it not necessarily because the movie was good but because the movie gave you something to measure and, in that measurement, a way to express yourself indirectly. When you rate the past, you can be certain that in the future you won't worry about having wasted time; you've been productive: You've created trends, and with enough trends, the future becomes predictable. As do you—and you end up knowing yourself better. That's not wishy-washy spiritual stuff—that's a sort of certainty, as in being more sure of your decisions so you can be more sure of how things will turn out or how they already did.

We made the bed into as best a copy of itself when we got there as we could, the duvet smoothed, the pillows fluffed; we dried our glasses; we didn't take out the trash. I put the travel-sized deodorant the host had left for me in my bag despite not having used it; I didn't want her to think of me as a stinky slob. In my text message letting her know I'd left, I made sure to say "I" not "we" after catching myself making the error in the first draft of the shower-curtain note I'd written earlier.

This was the digital version of Newport, albeit also a better version. I don't think it was better because it was digital, but that may have played a role. After all, that Newport guy would never have survived on Airbnb; the ratings would have crushed him.

How could someone live this way? my mom and I asked then, edge of judgment in our voices. How could someone let other people know he lives this way? we might ask today. The shock is not in how the person lives but in how the person serves others. The shock, now, would be that this man was risking his reputation.

My mom tells me she wouldn't have been totally honest in an online review of Newport because the dude was a friend of a friend. She would have left out the part about the bathtub, about the guy on the couch; she would have said the bed was an air mattress but not much more.

I thought of this while filling out the Airbnb review. If I reviewed my host, the email told me, I'd get to see her review of me. My obsession with reviews blocked me. I couldn't think of anything useful to say, even though everything had been pleasant. Though really it hadn't been—I'd just tricked myself, wanting the experience to seem perfect because a perfect experience would mean I made the correct choice. So I put the bed out of mind, ignored the doorbell because it seemed like a fluke. That left me with only nice things to say but no nice words with which to say them. There was no great way to describe neatness besides with the word "neat," no great way to describe the neighborhood's trees and quiet besides with the words "trees" and "quiet." So I turned to other reviews, borrowing the language of a "clean and welcoming" apartment with "great light" and an "easy to use kitchen."

Maybe the other reviewers borrowed too, all of us connected to the urtext of the host's description and photos, which showed off the way natural light pumped the room full of space, the orderly kitchen, the plush bed. We'd gotten what we wanted, which was what we'd been told we'd get. Reviews beget more reviews.

As with most online reviews, there were few three-star ones of the apartment. But even more than on Yelp and Amazon, where ratings cluster at the extremes, Airbnb ratings cluster just at the top—95 percent of the listings get four and a half or five stars—as if the fact of staying at someone's house tinges the transaction with the kind of interpersonal courteousness you'd use in real life, offline.

So I didn't mention the bed not only because I wanted to feel like I'd made a suitable choice of apartment but also because I didn't want to be rude, didn't want to mar an otherwise positive review with a negative that would stick out in a sea of uncomplaining five stars. Unlike hotels, which have name recognition, Airbnb hosts rely almost entirely on reviews to establish worth. As do their users. And as does Airbnb itself, which has a stake in making the transactions feel personal, because when they do, people are likely to be nicer— and when people are nicer, the reviews are better and Airbnb looks better too. The internet, despite all its trolls and threats, can sometimes be a place of structural positivity, where reputation is currency and the way to a good reputation is good reviews. Constant reviewing hasn't turned us into critics but cheerleaders.

Opening the review email from the host felt like opening a report card. In high school and middle school, I'd find my grades in the mail, stand next to the piano bench in the entryway to the house, heart fluttering, adrenaline dropping into my stomach. Every time I felt the same anxiety even though every time I knew pretty well how I'd do. But there was always some unknown—some ripped shower curtain—looming. And just as how I rated academically felt like a full description of me as a person, so did how I rated as a houseguest, one who hadn't even met the host. I knew both systems were rigged, but they were systems—systems that could justify the nervousness before and happiness after, systems that could validate the experience. And that was enough. It's the illusion that we're getting the full picture that has us trusting reviews at all, trusting these strangers to predict our experience because somehow, magically, by measuring, they've turned experience into an object, mass-produced and replicated, warranty not included.

I read the first sentence of the review in my phone's email-app preview: "Rachel was a fantastic guest!" Afraid that the start was a miscue, that the rest would mention the shower curtain and something I didn't even know I did wrong, it took me three more days to work up the nerve to actually open the email: "She took great care of my place and was great with communication. I highly recommend Rachel to all hosts!"

I could live with that. I had been good at texting her when I arrived and departed, and the note I left about the shower curtain was, I thought, suitably casual, without making light of the hole or forgetting to apologize. I'd done it—slept in a stranger's bed, lied about who else was in it, lied about a shower curtain—and still I was deemed a good communicator.

PRAISE

elene's hand feels like an antler. Her hand feels like I expect it to feel, but I don't expect what I do, which is squeeze hard and then let my hand turn to mush; she notices but doesn't say anything. Helene smiles in the elevator, smiles in the hallway, points to the bucket of compost outside her door. The door—her husband's name is still on it. When she asks what she can help me with, I say I'm not sure. Her husband's name is still on the door. Her husband is not home. When my husband was losing his mind, she starts a sentence. She starts a sentence. She sentences, doesn't start. I am startled by a draft; she closes the window. Helene tells me it's important to be honest with people. Helene tells me I have nothing to be ashamed of. Once when she stayed awake for a whole movie one of her friends praised her for being "good." Helene couldn't believe it in the way of "I can't believe it." I too couldn't believe it but I could because I too have been praised for being good, as if it's a behavior I can choose. And I too have been scolded for being bad, for having an early bedtime, for assuming. I presume everything. Helene tells me I can't assume people know what's going on. Helene tells me the worst was in the grocery store, fluorescent beams freezing her frozen body, a stroke of a stroke. Helene tells me it struck her late; she thought she was tired because she had so many kids. Helene tells me her kids are allowed to tell her she needs to take a nap. Helene tells me she doesn't like napping. Nor do I, because a nap requires waking. When Helene looks me in the eye and again tells me to have no shame, I cannot meet her gaze for more than a few seconds. It's dry in her apartment. *New Yorker* covers flutter in that same draft, back for another startling. A piano waits in the corner. My coat is on her coat rack. My legs are cramping but I must keep my shoes off her coffee table. Helene asks me when I found out. Helene asks if I was relieved after I ask her if she was relieved. So much in this unlit room glows. So much makes me want to close my eyes.

Helene asks me to do the math. Helene asks me to tell her what I think. Helene asks what medicine I take, if I know the brand names for her medicine. Helene feels no side effects. I tell her about my cold feet; it's important that people know about my cold feet. These are not a metaphor, these feet, these are a time for the word "literal."

BRIEFLY

n. Sleep lightly or briefly, especially during the day

woke to the suspicion that no one had texted me back, and I
was right.

I woke pawing at my phone, setting a new alarm from within the
half sleep the last one had barely dredged me from.

I woke to the woman across the aisle staring at me until I really woke
and focused and saw that she was staring out the window behind
me. I turned around to see what she saw: a train platform slipping
by, steam from commuters' noses and mouths clumped above the
wood platform, thinning.

I woke to some voice.

I woke to hands in my hands.

I woke alone.

I woke hungry.

I woke tired.

I woke in the confines of grammar, a sentence I couldn't remember burning the roof of my mouth. Was "to wake" transitive or intransitive? Could it mean to erase or to feel?

I woke thinking I was in a different room because I'd fallen asleep on the other side of my bed, too aggressively and quickly tired to move the laundry off the half I usually sleep on. Sometimes I force the end of a nap by dozing during laundry: Not wanting someone else to take my wet clothes out of the machine is a stronger desire than not wanting to wake up, but let me tell you, it's close. I've fallen asleep atop a heap of just-from-the-dryer clothes; I've fallen asleep on a bed with no sheets.

I woke to my watch vibrating on my wrist.

I woke to the memory of waking to roommates—the shrill clatter of plates on plates, the full thump of a pan hitting the sink, the faint hiss of heat and water.

I woke in darkness.

I woke to the part in the episode when the two people are shrieking at each other across the prison hallway from their separate cells. Had this been a nap, really? It had happened accidentally, and save for a quick relocation to my bedroom, it could have been part of the night's sleep. How important is intent? How important is your time awake before sleeping again?

I woke wondering why it was still Tuesday. Was there was any way for it not to be?

I woke dreading what I had to do next.

I woke to a spreadsheet that horrified not because it was a spreadsheet but because it meant I was at work. I had no intention of sleeping during the meeting, on the office couch, sunlight peering over my head, HVAC system jumping in and out of peripheral hearing, the perfect white-noise machine. We were there to discuss a very detailed yet boring process that involved formulas and keywords. But even if we'd been there to discuss my future husband, or my weekend plans, or what I would eat that night, or any of the things that take up an unnecessary and disproportionate amount of my thinking, there's no way I wouldn't have slipped off to sleep. Like stumbling up stairs, like dropping something for no good reason, it happened as if preordained. The velvet of the couch felt smooth or prickly, depending on which way I rubbed my hand against it. The woman's voice, as she talked to me, was authoritative or burdened, depending on which way I was moving—to or from sleep. Or I was authoritative or burdened, awake or asleep with feet planted firmly on the gray carpet pocked with pulled threads, as if it had been pressed over and over against Velcro.

I woke wrinkled.

I woke wondering if I would always be waking, if this is what day's material really is, just a series of moments you wake into, moments you're suddenly and unhappily aware of, moments that shock with their relentlessness.

I woke to it being time to go, always time to do something, often the something of not being asleep.

I woke to relief, to breathing, as I was not in the dream.

I woke helplessly; I woke helpless.

I woke on the sidewalk, face down, chipped tooth piece on my tongue, drunk out of my mind, unsure of everything.

I woke angry that I was awake, that I was no longer asleep.

I woke out of time: I woke to a sleep technician's voice, waking me from the third nap of my daytime sleep study. Each time I woke I knew exactly where I was—in a hospital room decorated as a bedroom. I tasted like night and looked like day gone wrong, with wires woven through hair, face creased by starchy sheets. Outside were the sharp taps of footsteps on thin carpet, and beyond that, the sharp ticks of rain on concrete. Every time I had a sleep study, there was the same collection of mini boxes of cereal, and I ate one after every nap, trudging down the hall, sensor box around my neck swaying side to side, to the combination kitchen-lounge, where I'd confront the bowl of small boxes and wait for their colors and mascots to jolt me awake. I was never jolted, only lulled back into sleepiness by the cereal itself. The problem was I wasn't allowed to sleep between naps, and so the day gained a kind of tension, split as it was between the pleasure of sleeping guilt-free during the day and the disarming pressure of, when I wasn't sleeping, time. The two hours between naps dragged. Then I was asleep, then as the door opened and I unpeeled a drool-stuck cheek from the sheets, I was awake. No one ever asked how I slept. I suppose it was against protocol. Instead, they asked, Did you sleep? And I wanted to say, You tell me. But I said, Yes, and waited in silence as I was untethered from the electronics. I felt, in those quiet moments, like a mannequin: dressed in clothes that didn't quite fit, with a single purpose. Which, in my case, was to do as I was told and go to sleep and wake up according to a decades-old pattern so someone could look at my sleep and find in it its own pattern.

I woke wishing I could make statements like hers—sentences that held meaning and sounded like what they meant.

I woke waking, shrieking back into the day, an easing incessantly rough as I tumbled back into light and felt in the opening of my eyes the closing of accomplishment.

I woke decontextualized.

I woke cradling a book.

I woke to arms still asleep.

I woke to dashed hopes, the day-sleep splattered, the cold of my bedroom exaggerated by the darkness that wasn't there when I fell asleep. The timeline was as uniform as ever. I'm told I nap for too long, that by letting myself go into deep sleep, I'm risking sleep inertia, that awful postnap malaise that makes me feel like long-awaited plans have just fallen through, like I've just been dumped.

I woke two minutes before my alarm was set to go off—that is, I woke disappointed.

I woke in the memory of waking from those early naps, when they seemed a symptom of being a senior in high school, not of unexplainable exhaustion. I still cram sleep into the day's crevices, end it an hour or so after it begins, cold and vaulted.

I woke in silence.

I woke panicked.

I woke groaning.

I woke in all my clothes and remembered the rush I was in to fall asleep as quickly as possible after work and before dinner, forestalling the rest of the day. A version of this was once routine: On Fridays I'd come home from work, hope my roommates weren't there to make small talk with, and duck into my room, where I'd tear off my pants and leap into bed. I would've already chosen my nap 1, nap 2, or nap 3 alarm on the train, given what time it was, leaving enough space postnap to take a wake-up shower, eat, and start drinking before heading out for the night. This nap, so well-intentioned, so thoroughly planned and rehearsed, never elicited guilt, only grogginess. Now I get home later, and the naps are shorter, and I wake when a counting-down timer goes off, not an alarm. For these naps, I lie flat on my back, my hair carefully pressed straight against the pillow so I'll look the same when I wake as I did when I fell asleep. These are the naps I take with all my clothes on, on my bed atop the covers and under my nap blanket, a perpetually hair-covered maroon fleece that used to be my grandmother's.

I woke like a hangnail still hanging; I woke as a nagging annoyance waiting to be chewed off and thrown behind the couch or into the trash.

I woke gutted, and I stumbled to the kitchen to fill myself back up.

I woke to a trill glitching from my phone, tangled and tingly as I tried to gently tap the screen.

I woke like a lousy startup.

I woke sure it was the next day, sure that my nap had turned into sleep. But where is the difference? Is it in length alone? Is it in the particular hour, minute, second of day? Every definition has its gray areas—a long nap could be a sleep-deprived person's sleep, a night-shift worker could nap in the early morning. Is it how you feel when you wake up?—dreading the day ahead or dreading what little of it there is left. Maybe it's in how you feel about what you just did—whether you resent the activity for not living up to expectations and resent yourself for having those expectations in the first place. How close "reset" is to "resent" and "rest" is an accident: I hope beforehand and I wake to something real and different after; I've never been happy to wake from a nap.

I woke to a nap stretched thin by a loud radiator that thickened the air molasses-sweet and sulfuric.

I woke more tired than I was before.

I woke into waking, into the dream of the perfect nap: beneath a blanket, on a couch, with a pillow from a bed that I don't need to put back on the bed after the nap, with the lights out and the sun shining on my body but not on my face, a little chilly outside of the blanket but warm when I wake up, with a snack of digestives and chocolate chips waiting in the kitchen, right before dinner before going out, in a position that doesn't smoosh my hair, for as long as I need to sleep but without actually stealing time from the day, without a nagging feeling that I might at some point during the nap have to pee, without a nagging suspicion that someone will see me asleep, without any doubt about what I will do after the nap and with the promise of those plans being fun, on a Friday before a Saturday on which I can sleep in and get a pastry.

I woke useless, uselessly.

I woke knowing what I'd said had backfired.

I woke snubbed by my personal equation: Why didn't one hour asleep make me feel one hour more rested? When two astronomers measure the transit of the same celestial body and they come up with different numbers, the discrepancy arises from their personal equations—their sets of biases and reaction times and everything else that tinges the objective with the subjective. I was those two astronomers in one body; I was biased toward sleep and away from it.

I woke where I'd begun, past the lines of sunlight let in by the drawn blinds whose slats shimmied in radiator-lifted air.

I woke to a room of applause, and I was applauding too, on my feet for the apparently wonderful talk Salman Rushdie had just given at my college.

I woke to a chase scene.

I woke midsentence: a description of the house being renovated, its naked beams letting the cold in.

I woke to the woman next to me at work asleep, her sleep deep and unselfconscious, the opposite of my brief and frenzied foray. I want desperately to know whether anyone else notices her, head down on arms, lips parted, keyboard centered above her head. She is mostly hidden by screens, but if you look closely, where her neck curves and her shoulders round, you can see the soft up and down of her breathing. Sometimes she's more obvious: Facing away from the computer, toward the windows, afternoon light seeping through the clouds, she leans back in her desk chair and looks unhappy but as if she would be even less happy awake. Her arms hang straight down, and her fingers curl limply into the weak clutch of someone watched by no one, unaware and unassuming. Whenever she does this, I scoff, turn to look to my left, each time looking away quickly for fear that she'll snap awake to me staring at her. She shouldn't be allowed, I seethe, because we all should be allowed, we should all be facing the windows, asleep postlunch and slack with the workplace irresponsibility of it. I scoff, in other words, because I'm jealous. I'm so jealous, and I'm so tired. I want to be slouched with open mouth in public, at work, but even more, I want to do so unnoticed, fading into invisibility as I fade out of consciousness, disappearing so I'm not an anomaly of the waking day or a repository of daytime nightmares but, simply, nothing, nowhere, not a worker shirking her responsibility and getting paid to sleep, not a person missing out on anything, not a spectacle. But I'm far from achieving that, and this woman who sits next to me hasn't achieved that yet, because here I am spectating, nervous she'll get found out.

I woke as my hands loosened their grip on my book and the hardcover levered into my thumbs.

I woke dappled.

I woke held.

I woke beheld.

I woke upset that the dream wasn't real, that we weren't in his car on our way to a weekend vacation in the woods. But then I fell back to sleep and this time when I woke I woke relieved: We had not really just broken up because we had, in waking life, never dated in the first place.

I woke giving in.

I woke worried I had not napped for long enough.

I woke midsentence—my own.

ACKNOWLEDGMENTS

Thank you:

John D'Agata, for reading my essays aloud; Catherine Imbriglio, for teaching me; Kerry Howley, for your guidance; Robyn Schiff, for your generosity;

the Iowa Arts Fellowship and Friends of Lakeside Lab Writing Fellowship, for the luxury of writing;

Spenser Mestel, for your reasoned approach; Liz Parker, for your optimism; Gemma de Choisy, for saying "measurement";

Sarah Gorham, for believing this possible; Ariel Lewiton, for seeing promise; Samantha Shea, for shepherding this book;

Ben Hyman, for your sincerity; Kate Taylor, for your laughter; Ryan Grubbs, for your calm;

M and D, for your love.

Earlier versions of some of these essays appeared in *Entropy*, *Quartz*, *The Believer Logger*, and *Woolly*.

SOURCES

Aldrich, Michael. *Sleep Medicine*. New York: Oxford University Press, 1999.

Aristotle. *Aristotle: Selections*. Translated by Terence Irwin and Gail Fine. Indianapolis: Hackett Publishing, 1995.

Ashbery, John. *Hotel Lautréamont*. New York: Knopf, 1992.

Ashdown, Susan. *Sizing in Clothing: Developing Effective Sizing Systems for Ready to Wear Clothing*. Cambridge: Woodhead Publishing Limited, 2007.

Barmann, Kit. "Purchasing Power of Women." *FONA International* (blog). December 22, 2014. http://www.fona.com/resource-center/blog /purchasing-power-women.

Blaivas, Allen. "Polysomnography." *A.D.A.M. Medical Encyclopedia* entry, MedlinePlus online database. Accessed July 1, 2015. https://medlineplus .gov/ency/article/003932.htm.

Boater Exam. "Very Superstitious: 13 Sailor Superstitions." *Boating Safety and Safe Boating Blog*. July 15, 2011. http://www.boaterexam.com /blog/2011/07/boater-superstitions.aspx.

Boorady, Lynn (chair, Fashion and Textile Technology, State University of New York–Buffalo). Phone interview by author. September 2015.

Brookhouse, Brent. "Dana White Talks Ronda Rousey's Appeal: 'She's Like A Dude Trapped In This Beautiful Body.'" SB Nation. *Bloody Elbow* (blog), September 17, 2012. http://www.bloodyelbow.com/2012/9/17/3347658 /dana-white-ronda-rousey-in-ufc-strikeforce.

Carskadon, Mary A., and William C. Dement. "Sleepiness and Sleep State on a 90-Min Schedule." *Psychophysiology* 14, no. 2 (March 1977): 127-133.

———. "Sleep Studies on a 90-Minute Day." *Electroencephalography and Clinical Neurophysiology* 39, no. 2 (August 1975): 145-155.

Chayka, Kyle. "Here's How to Predict the Weather Using Your Cat." Time.com, February 17, 2014. http://time.com/8165/heres-how-to -predict-the-weather-using-your-cat/.

Chen, Lichao, Ritchie E. Brown, James T. McKenna, and Robert W. McCarley. "Animal Models of Narcolepsy." *CNS & Neurological Disorders: Drug Targets* 8, no. 4 (2009): 296-308.

Christenson, Clayton M. *The Innovator's Dilemma: When New Technologies Cause Great Firms to Fail*. Boston: Harvard Business Review Press, 1997.

Clairambault, Jean, Stephane Gaubert, and Thomas Lepoutre. "Circadian Rhythm and Cell Population Growth." *Mathematical and Computer Modelling* 53, no. 7–8 (April 2011): 1558-1567.

Cuordileone, K. A. *Manhood and American Political Culture in the Cold War*. New York: Routledge, 2005.

Daniels, Cora Linn, and C. M. Stevans, eds. *Encyclopaedia of Superstitions, Folklore, and the Occult Sciences of the World*, Vol. 2. Facsimile of the 1903 edition. Detroit: Gale Research, 1971.

De La Peña, Carolyn. "The Origins of Cybex Space." *Cabinet Magazine* 29 (Spring 2008). http://www.cabinetmagazine.org/issues/29/pena.php.

Dillon, Charles Raymond. *Superstitions and Folk Remedies*. San Jose: Authors Choice Press, 2001.

Division of Sleep Medicine at Harvard Medical School. "Healthy Sleep: Natural Patterns of Sleep." Accessed December 18, 2007. http://healthysleep .med.harvard.edu/healthy/science/what/sleep-patterns-rem-nrem.

———. "Healthy Sleep: The Characteristics of Sleep." Accessed December 18, 2007. http://healthysleep.med.harvard.edu/healthy/science/what /characteristics.

———. "Healthy Sleep: Why Do We Sleep Anyway?" Accessed December 18, 2007. http://healthysleep.med.harvard.edu/healthy/matters /benefits-of-sleep/why-do-we-sleep.

———. "Narcolepsy: Medications." Accessed July 22, 2013. http://healthysleep .med.harvard.edu/narcolepsy/treating-narcolepsy/medications.

———. "Narcolepsy: The Science of Narcolepsy." Accessed July 19, 2013. http://healthysleep.med.harvard.edu/narcolepsy/what-is-narcolepsy /science-of-narcolepsy.

Dombek, Kristin. *The Selfishness of Others: An Essay on the Fear of Narcissism*. New York: Farrar, Straus and Giroux, 2016.

DSM Pharmaceuticals Inc. "Adderall (CII)." Drugs@FDA: FDA Approved Drug Products database. PDF. March 2007. https://www.accessdata .fda.gov/drugsatfda_docs/label/2007/011522s040lbl.pdf.

Felsenthal, Julia. "A Size 2 Is a Size 2 Is a Size 8." *Slate*, January 25, 2012. http:// www.slate.com/articles/arts/design/2012/01/clothing_sizes_getting _bigger_why_our_sizing_system_makes_no_sense_.html.

Finger, Stanley. *Origins of Neuroscience: A History of Explorations Into Brain Function.* Oxford: Oxford University Press, 1994.

Flood, Karen P. "Bodybuilding." In *American Masculinities: A Historical Encyclopedia*, edited by Bret Carroll, 59-60. Thousand Oaks, CA: Sage Publications, 2003.

Foer, Joshua. "The Adderall Me." *Slate*, May 10, 2005. http://www.slate .com/articles/health_and_science/medical_examiner/2005/05 /the_adderall_me.html.

Frederick, Christine. *The New Housekeeping: Efficiency Studies in Home Management.* Garden City, NY: Doubleday, Page & Company, 1913.

Frederickson, Barbara L., and Daniel Kahneman. "Duration Neglect in Retrospective Evaluations of Affective Episodes." *Journal of Personality and Social Psychology* 65, no. 1 (July 1993): 45-55.

Jacobs, Alan. "The Lost World of Benzedrine." *Atlantic*, April 2012.

Jazz Pharmaceuticals. "Office Support: The Xyrem REMS Program." Accessed June 1, 2017. https://www.xyrem.com/healthcare-professionals/xyrem -prescriber-tools.

John F. Kennedy Library Foundation. "The Federal Government Takes on Physical Fitness." *JFK in History*. Accessed June 1, 2017. https://www .jfklibrary.org/JFK/JFK-in-History/Physical-Fitness.aspx.

Johns, M. "A New Method for Measuring Daytime Sleepiness: The Epworth Sleepiness Scale." *Sleep* 14, no. 6 (December 1991): 540-545.

Johnson, Clifton. "Some New England Superstitions." *New England Magazine* 35 (1906-1907): 161-168.

Johnson, H. H. "Birds as Prognosticators." *The Osprey* 3, no. 9 (May 1899): 134-135.

Jones, Matt. "Ronda Rousey Offered $100,000 Fight Challenge by UFC Legend Tank Abbott." *Bleacher Report*, September 22, 2015. http:// bleacherreport.com/articles/2570539-ronda-rousey-offered-100000 -fight-challenge-by-ufc-legend-tank-abbott.

Kahneman, Daniel, Barbara L. Fredrickson, Charles A. Schreiber, and Donald A. Redelmeier. "When More Pain is Preferred to Less: Adding a Better End." *Psychological Science* 4, no. 6 (1993): 401-405.

Kennedy, John F. "The Soft American." *Sports Illustrated*, December 26, 1960.

Kryger, Meir, Thomas Roth, and William Dement. *Principles and Practice of Sleep Medicine*. Philadelphia, Elsevier: 2016

Land, Leslie. "How the Marketing of Modernism Hijacked the Kitchen Stove." In *From Betty Crocker to Feminist Food Studies: Critical Perspectives on Women and Food*, edited by Arlene Voski Avakian and Barbara Haber, 41-61. Amherst, MA: University of Massachusetts Press, 2005.

Long, L., J. Faraco, R. Li, et al. "The Sleep Disorder Canine Narcolepsy Is Caused by a Mutation in the Hypocretin (Orexin) Receptor 2 Gene." *Cell* 98, no. 3 (August 1999): 365-376.

Lusk, Graham. "The Fundamental Requirements of Energy for Proper Nutrition." *Journal of the American Medical Association* 70, no. 12. (1918): 821-824.

Lynch, Gerald. "The Real Reason Netflix Won't Offer Offline Downloads." *Gizmodo*, September 7, 2015. http://gizmodo.com/the-real-reason -netflix-wont-offer-offline-downloads-1729146143.

Massachusetts General Hospital. "Advanced EEG Analysis Reveals the Complex Beauty of the Sleeping Brain." News release, February 7, 2017. http://www.massgeneral.org/News/pressrelease.aspx?id=2055.

Matchar, Emily. *Homeward Bound: Why Women Are Embracing the New Domesticity*. New York: Simon and Schuster, 2013.

MMA Chicas. "Ronda Rousey vs Cat Zingano Full Fight. The Fastest WIN Ever!" Filmed February 28, 2015. YouTube video, 0:30. Posted July 5, 2015. https://www.youtube.com/watch?v=If8j5vIEbXk.

National Institute of Neurological Disorders and Stroke. "Brain Basics: Understanding Sleep." Accessed July 1, 2015. http://www.ninds.nih.gov /disorders/brain_basics/understanding_sleep.htm.

National Institute on Drug Abuse. "How Do Stimulants Affect the Brain and Body?" *Misuse of Prescription Drugs: Research Report Series.* August 2016. https://www.drugabuse.gov/publications/research-reports /prescription-drugs/stimulants/how-do-stimulants-affect-brain-body.

National Sleep Foundation. "What Happens When You Sleep?" Accessed July 1, 2015. https://sleepfoundation.org/how-sleep-works/what -happens-when-you-sleep.

National Weather Service. "How Lightning Is Created." Accessed June 1, 2017. http://www.srh.noaa.gov/jetstream/lightning/lightning.html.

O'Brien, Ruth, and William Shelton. *Women's Measurements for Garment and Pattern Construction*. Washington: Government Printing Office, 1941.

Pollak, Charles, Michael Thorpy, and Jan Yager. *The Encyclopedia of Sleep and Sleep Disorders*, 3rd ed. New York: Infobase Publishing, 2010.

Powell, Alvin. "America's First Time Zone." *Harvard Gazette*, November 10, 2011. http://news.harvard.edu/gazette/story/2011/11/americas -first-time-zone/.

Quirk, Mary Beth. "Netflix Won't Offer Downloadable Content Anytime Soon Because Users Just Couldn't Handle It." *Consumerist*, September 8, 2015. https://consumerist.com/2015/09/08/netflix-wont-offer -downloadable-content-anytime-soon-because-users-just-couldnt -handle-it/.

Rasmussen, Nicolas. "America's First Amphetamine Epidemic 1929–1971: A Quantitative and Qualitative Retrospective with Implications for the Present." *American Journal of Public Health* 98, no. 6 (June 2008): 974-985.

Rodriguez, Ashley. "Netflix Is Nixing Its Old Star-Rating System for One You Might Actually Use." *Quartz*, March 17, 2017. https://qz.com/935464 /netflix-nflx-is-nixing-its-old-star-rating-system.

Roper, William. *Weather Sayings, Proverbs and Prognostics, Chiefly from North Lancashire*. Lancaster: Thomas Bell and Co. Printers, 1883.

Rousey, Ronda. Ronda Jean Rousey: MMA, Actress, Judo. Webpage. Accessed June 1, 2017. https://rondarousey.net/about. See esp. section 3, "Olympic Judo Career."

Sanford, E. C. "Personal Equation." *American Journal of Psychology* 2, no. 1 (November 1888): 3-38.

Segall, Ken. *Think Simple: How Smart Leaders Defeat Complexity*. New York: Portfolio/Penguin, 2016.

Shire. "Medication Guide: Adderall XR." Drugs@FDA: FDA Approved Drug Products database. PDF. March 2007. https://www.accessdata.fda.gov /drugsatfda_docs/label/2007/021303s015lbl.pdf.

Shteyngart, Gary. *Super Sad True Love Story*. New York: Random House, 2010.

Siegel, Jerome. *The Neural Control of Sleep and Waking*. New York: Springer, 2002.

Siegel, J. M., R. Moore, T. Thannickal, and R. Nienhuis. "A Brief History of Hypocretin/Orexin and Narcolepsy." *Neuropyschopharmacology* 25, S5 (2001): S14-S20.

Stern, Marc. "The Fitness Movement and the Fitness Center Industry." *Business and Economic History Online* 6 (2008): 1-26.

Stern, Marlow. "The Rise of 'Rowdy' Ronda Rousey: The 14-Second Assassin." *Daily Beast*, March 11, 2015. http://www.thedailybeast.com

/articles/2015/03/11/the-rise-of-rowdy-ronda-rousey-the-14-second
-assassin.html.

Stone, Alex. "Why Waiting Is Torture." *New York Times*, August 18, 2012.
http://www.nytimes.com/2012/08/19/opinion/sunday/why-waiting-in
-line-is-torture.html?_r=0.

Thorpy, Michael J., and Michel Billiard. *Sleepiness: Causes, Consequences and
Treatment*. Cambridge: Cambridge University Press, 2011.

UCLA Health. "Patient Education: Circadian Rhythms." Accessed June 1,
2017. http://sleepcenter.ucla.edu/circadian-rhythms.

UFC - Ultimate Fighting Championship. "UFC 184: Cat Zingano Octagon
Interview." Filmed February 28, 2015. YouTube video, 1:37. Posted
February 28, 2015. https://www.youtube.com/watch?v=gRxDguNMl7w.

UFC - Ultimate Fighting Championship. "UFC 184: Ronda Rousey Octagon
Interview." Filmed February 28, 2015. YouTube video, 1:44. Posted February
28, 2015. https://www.youtube.com/watch?v=LDRKbHQNXmM.

Ultimate Fighting Championship. "Cat Zingano." Fighter page. Accessed
June 1, 2017. http://www.ufc.com/fighter/cat-Zingano?id.

US Department of Health and Human Services. "President's Council on
Fitness, Sports & Nutrition: Our History." August 9, 2017. https://www
.hhs.gov/fitness/about-pcfsn/our-history/.

Webster, Richard. *The Encyclopedia of Superstitions*. Woodbury, MN:
Llewellyn Publications, 2008.

WGBH Boston. "A Social History of America's Most Popular Drugs."
Web content in support of *Frontline* episodes "Drug Wars." Episodes
aired October 9, 2000, and October 10, 2000. Accessed June 1, 2017.
http://www.pbs.org/wgbh/pages/frontline/shows/drugs/buyers
/socialhistory.html.

Wright, C. D. "Girl Friend Poem #10." In *Steal Away: Selected and New Poems*,
193. Port Townshend, WA: Copper Canyon Press, 2003.

Zervas, Georgios, Davide Proserpio, and John Byers. "A First Look at Online
Reputation on Airbnb, Where Every Stay Is Above Average." *Social
Science Research Network*, April 12, 2015. http://papers.ssrn.com/sol3
/papers.cfm?abstract_id=2554500.

SARABANDE BOOKS is a nonprofit literary press located in Louisville, KY. Founded in 1994 to champion poetry, short fiction, and essay, we are committed to creating lasting editions that honor exceptional writing. For more information, please visit sarabandebooks.org.